PRACTICAL ENGLISH GRAMMAR
FOR
ACADEMIC WRITERS

Kenneth Cranker

WAYZGOOSE PRESS

Practical English Grammar for Academic Writers
Copyright © 2018 by Wayzgoose Press

ISBN: 978-1-938757-40-2

Text by Kenneth Cranker
Edited by Dorothy E. Zemach
Book design by DJ Rogers Design
Published in the United States by Wayzgoose Press

Foreword

This textbook springs from a short course (12-14 hours) called Advanced Grammar in Writing that I designed and have taught at the University of Delaware English Language Institute since 2012. The course was designed to be of maximal assistance to pre-university students of English who are dealing with academic content but still struggling somewhat with grammar in their academic writing.

The strategy was to cover a broad range of grammar yet to limit it to that which is useful in academic writing. To maximize the impact, special attention was given to the most common errors, both at word level and sentence level, that seem to plague the writing seen at the upper levels of the Institute.

The resulting course has been quite successful over the years at helping students meet the standards of writing necessary to matriculate to the university, and the teaching has been evaluated positively by the students. Recently, one student commented, "You should make a book that contains the things you've taught us in this class." This textbook is the attempt to do just that.

This book, because it is compact, focuses almost exclusively on academic written grammar, and is written primarily with academic vocabulary and style, is ideal for pre-university writing classes in which academic reading and writing are emphasized, but where some focus on grammar is also needed.
It also contains an answer key, so students can study this material autonomously. The answer key includes model paragraphs for every paragraph writing exercise. These sample responses not only offer students ideas for their own writing, but also model an academic style of writing that students an absorb by reading them. Concepts from a breadth of academic fields are presented, so using this book will also foster the development of academic vocabulary.

I would like to acknowledge Emi Cranker for her invaluable assistance with the original formatting this text. Her patience and skill made this text much more eye-appealing than it was when I originally created it. Many thanks to the talented DJ Rogers who made the manuscript suitable for publication.

Ken Cranker

Table of Contents

Unit 1 Sentence Focus

Perhaps the greatest need for transformation among writers preparing for university study is to write sentences that focus on concepts (and are therefore more academic and impersonal) and paragraphs that are cohesive in their focus. This focus on *focus* will be an important recurring theme in this textbook. Consider the following, a typical piece of student writing about the need to reduce pollution.

Paragraph 1

People drive cars every day to school, to work and to play. These cars give off gases that pollute the air and can make people sick. Because governments are responsible for protecting their citizens, they should pass stricter laws to reduce the gases that automobiles give off.

Notice the subjects of the sentences: *people*, *cars*, *they* (*governments*). Looking at only the subjects of the sentences, it would be very difficult to guess what this paragraph is about. In fact, what *is* the paragraph about? Pollution, right? However, pollution is never actually mentioned (although the verb *pollute* is), so this paragraph requires readers to infer meaning. It is not well-focused.

Now consider this refocused revision.

Paragraph 2

Air pollution is a serious issue facing governments today. A primary factor of this pollution is emissions from automobiles. Exhaust fumes from cars contain chemicals that lead to illnesses such as lung cancer and emphysema[1]. Thus, strict government regulation of emissions is warranted[2] to ensure reduction of harmful pollutants and the protection of the health of citizens.

Notice the subjects of the sentences: *pollution*, *factor* (of pollution), *exhaust fumes* (= pollution), (government) *regulation* (of emissions = pollution). It is far easier to determine what this paragraph is about.

It also sounds considerably more academic, doesn't it? How is this improvement achieved? By focusing on the concept (*pollution*), using synonyms that refer back to that concept, and by **nominalizing**. Nominalization is the process of making nouns from other parts of speech to refer to a concept or process. Nominalization will also be addressed again later in this book. This is just a short introduction.

---

1 emphysema: a lung disease
2 warranted: called for, necessary

- pollution (from the verb *pollute*)
- emissions (from the verb *emit*, which means "*give off*")
- illnesses (from the adjective *ill*, which means "*being sick*")
- regulation (from the verb *regulate*, which means "*pass stricter laws*")
- reduction (from the verb *reduce*),
- protection (from the verb *protect*, from which also comes the gerund *protecting*)

Clearly, nominalization improves focus and boosts vocabulary level, resulting in writing that is more acceptable at the university level. There is much more on nominalization in Unit 6.

✓ **Writing tip:** Improve focus and boost the vocabularly level of academic writing by nominalizing.

Exercise 1

Nominalize a word in the following sentences and make it the subject to improve focus and/or boost vocabulary. The first has been done for you.

a. People wanted better jobs, so they immigrated to the U.S.
   Immigrants came to the U.S. seeking employment.

b. People from Europe enabled the U.S. to expand westward.

c. America could not have industrialized without new people to work in factories.

d. The people who came to America tended to be rugged[3] and individualistic, and that caused American culture to also be individualistic.

e. Immigrants were also patriotic[4] toward their new home, which made America stronger.

f. These days many people come to the U.S. to be educated.

Exercise 2

Write a short paragraph focusing on the roles of immigrants/immigration in the U.S. Some subtopics might include expansion, industrialization, patriotism, education, or individualism.

---

3 rugged: strong, tough
4 patriotic: loving one's country

Unit 2 Triads

Triads, or groups of three, while more stylistic than grammatical, can dramatically improve the feeling of academic writing. Generally speaking, a paragraph is not considered a paragraph unless it has at least three sentences. The traditional 5-paragraph essay that many have been taught, and which may be going out of fashion, was considered sufficiently developed because it contained three body paragraphs. A group of three has a complete, developed, mature sense to it. (Did you notice the adjectival triad in the previous sentence?)

Why three? What's so wonderful about three? Is it magical? (Did you notice the triad of three questions?) No, it is probably not magical. Depending on the genre, compositions may have more or fewer than three main paragraphs. Paragraphs may certainly have more than three sentences. Adjectival expressions also do not have to contain three adjectives. (Did you notice the triad: *compositions*, *paragraphs*, and *adjectival expressions*?) Nevertheless, there is a balanced, stable, and almost poetic feeling that triads communicate subliminally. But why?

It may result from the fact that the human mind is conditioned to the world around it. The world is three-dimensional (length, width, and height). It consists of three major geographical constituents[5]: land, water, and air. In a somewhat related manner, matter exists in three phases: solid, liquid, and gas. Time is usually divided into past, present, and future. A family traditionally consists of mother, father, and child(ren). Of course families vary, but the fundamental notion of family that perpetuates[6] the race is a triad. (Incidentally, I went beyond a triad with my examples of triads. Did it feel excessive? I could have listed many more.) Whatever the reason, triads are effective in raising the academic feel of writing.

✓ **Writing tip:** When using triads, parallel structure is of utmost importance. The three parts of the triad must be expressed in the same grammatical structure (all nouns, all adjectives, all that clauses, for example). Parallel structure is an essential element of effective writing, and it will be another recurring theme in this text.

Exercise 1

The following message was taken with permission from the 2016 Newsletter from the English Language Institute (ELI) at the University of Delaware in the US. The title is *From the Director's Desk*. The director is a respected, well-published academic writer. Read it and identify the triads used. Some triads are easily identifiable, and some are relatively subtle[7]. You may be surprised at how many you find.

---

5 constituents: parts
6 perpetuates: continues
7 subtle: hard to notice

Dear ELI Friend,

It is my distinct pleasure both to greet our students when they arrive and to congratulate them at graduation, with, of course, many encounters in between. Almost invariably[8], I find that the fluent student confidently shaking my hand on graduation day bears little resemblance to the shy, mono-lingual new arrival I welcomed months earlier during orientation. In the course of time, a radical transformation has taken place, one that transcends[9] the simple acquisition of second language skills. You see, assuming the role of international student is not simply about learning; it's also about becoming. The sojourn from China, Oman, or Colombia does not end with the unpacking of bags in Newark; rather, ELI becomes the point of departure on a deeper journey to the center of the soul. To study in a foreign land is to embark on a quest for identity.

Consider the case of Shingo, an ELI student from Japan. Speaking Japanese while still in Tokyo, Shingo knew himself and was at ease within the protocols and nuances[10] of his culture. But here in Newark, English opens a door, not simply to new words, but to an uncharted world of uncertain-ty. Should he bow or shake hands? Should he look down or make eye contact? Does he preserve his silence and humility or embrace the loud, self-promoting exuberance[11] of his American peers? Finding himself in this new world is like learning to dance to a strange new rhythm. At times, Shingo feels lost and anonymous, no longer certain of his Japanese identity, while simultaneously sensing he is an imposter among Americans. As the months pass, however, Shingo begins to find his footing—coming to treasure more deeply the beauty, order, and elegance of Japanese traditions and also finding himself more at ease within the looser, freer, more fluid dimensions of American culture. He has learned to love and live in two worlds.

This year's edition of our annual newsletter captures how ELI helps students like Shingo evolve into global citizens. The first mark of becoming a global citizen is acquiring the English proficiency to bridge the linguistic divide among classmates from 35 different countries, including, the U.S. The second set of competencies is the ability and willingness to traverse cultural barriers, searching for commonalities and celebrating differences. Navigating the sometimes tempestuous[12] waters of cul-tural conflicts requires patience, empathy, and the courage to set aside time-worn narratives long enough to listen and, perhaps, together write a new story. As Marcel Proust observed, "The real voyage of discovery consists not in finding new landscapes, but in having new eyes."

In the end, however, global citizenship is more than language and cultural understanding; rather it is casting the net of concern and compassion beyond one's borders.

It's Saudi scholars going to Puerto Rico to repair homes for the poor; it's a Rwandan professional raising awareness among University of Delaware undergraduates of human rights abuses and the subsequent healing power of forgiveness and reconciliation[13]; it's a Syrian artist collaborating with

---

8 invariably: always
9 transcends: crosses, exceeds
10 nuances: subtle meanings
11 exuberance: enthusiasm
12 tempestuous: rough, stormy
13 reconciliation: restoring relationships

University of Delaware dancers to tell the tragic story of Aleppo, infusing pain with hope. Inside these covers, you will discover remarkable students whose search for identity through their ELI experience proved to be transformative, not only for themselves, but for others as well. Enjoy.

Sincerely,

Exercise 2

Use triads to describe the following. The first two are done for you.

a. The weather: *Summer weather here is typically hazy, hot, and humid.*

b. Your computer: *My computer is old, slow, and unreliable.*

c. How you feel today: _____

d. Your favorite course: _____

e. Why English is difficult: _____

f. Favorite foods: _____

g. Common excuses for being late: ___ _____

Unit 3 Verb Tenses

In practical academic writing, there are really only four verb tenses commonly used: the simple present, the present continuous, the present perfect, and the simple past. While the future tense is also used, it is debatable whether technically it really is a tense – because the verb is not modified at all; *will*, a modal, is merely added. This textbook will forego[14] addressing the future tense, as it is so simple, but it will focus on the other four.

A. SIMPLE PRESENT

There are two very common errors with the present tense: not forming it properly by forgetting to add the *–s/-es* to the 3rd person singular, and not realizing the "always-ness" it implies. At the advanced level, forgetting the *–s/-es* is not a matter of ignorance. Students know they should add it; they just do not do it. They tend to write the way they speak. Thus, this habit can be overcome by intensive oral feedback and proofreading practice. Reading about it in a book is not likely to fix the problem.

However, progress in correcting the second type of error can be achieved by considering the following sentence, which students I have taught generally consider acceptable.

> 1. The Chinese economy grows rapidly.   X

The implication of this sentence is that the Chinese economy always grows rapidly; it has in the past, it does now, and it will in the future. It is analogous[15] to the sentence

> 2. He likes bananas.

He always likes bananas, past, present, and future. His taste for bananas does not change. Can that be said of the Chinese economy? Has it always grown? Is it growing now? Will it always grow in the future? No. Therefore, this use of the present tense is incorrect.

How, then, can sentence 1 be corrected? Different tenses must be employed.

> 3. The Chinese economy is growing rapidly. (present continuous)
> 4. The Chinese economy has grown rapidly since it incorporated Hong Kong. (present perfect)
> 5. The Chinese economy has been growing rapidly for the last two decades (present perfect continuous – less common).

---

14 forego: skip
15 be analogous: be similar to something

Exercise 1

Which of the following sentences are correct? How can the erroneous ones be fixed?

a. DNA determines which proteins a cell makes.
b. The market share of Brand ABC expands.
c. Computers simplify creating documents.
d. Global temperatures rise since 2000.
e. Tulips lose popularity in Georgia.
f. The topic I choose for my research paper is Internet censorship[16].

Exercise 2

Proofread the following paragraph for errors with the simple present tense. Discuss what you found with a partner or group.

Chen is a student from China preparing for college in the United States. He face many difficulties. He report that simply getting out of bed is difficult because of jet lag. His body clock does not seem to work properly. As a result, he often miss his first class, so he is on academic probation. Another problem he have is that he struggles with daily responsibilities such as fixing meals and cleaning his room. Not eating well make him tired, so he cannot pay attention in class, and living in a dirty room cause him to be unproductive, which lead to lower grades. He does not pass his classes this session.

This paragraph is about a particular Chinese student, which leads to the use of 3rd person singular present tense verbs. If the paragraph had been written about difficulties that most international students face, subjects would be pluralized, meaning no –s/-es would be needed for verbs.

> ✓ **Writing tip:** Write general statements in the plural to facilitate[17] the use of verbs and to eliminate the need for *he/she* pronoun choices.

---

16 censorship: strict government regulation of speech
17 facilitate: make easier

Exercise 3

Read the following paragraph and highlight how the present tense is properly used.

American college students tend to display speaking habits that often perplex[18] international students. They speak quickly, use slang or vulgar language, and fail to use intonation patterns similar to those of English teachers. Even when internationals excel in their college prep English classes, they still struggle when interacting with American students for the above reasons. English teachers cannot be faulted for speaking more slowly, in standard language, or with proper intonation to communicate meaning. Their job is to teach. The difficulty is mostly attributable to the unique adolescent[19] culture on college campuses. Most college graduates tend to speak in a manner more similar to that of English teachers once they are employed and are compelled to communicate with colleagues older than themselves.

Exercise 4

Choose one of the following topics and write a paragraph of your own.

a. Describe habits of one or both of your parents.
b. Describe how most commuters travel to work in your country.
c. Compare and contrast breakfast in your country with breakfast in the U.S.

B. PRESENT CONTINUOUS

The present continuous tense is used to describe something that is currently happening. In academic writing, it is often used to describe trends. The tense is constructed by *be*-verb + verb + –*ing*.

1. Gasoline prices are rising.
2. Global temperatures also seem to be increasing.
3. That politician is considering various policies to counteract these troubling trends.

Advanced students may occasionally forget the *be*-verb portion of the present continuous tense, but this error is relatively rare. More serious is the confusion between the present and the present continuous as described in the simple present section.

18 perplex: confuse
19 adolescent: teenage

a. Construct a triad describing what is happening around you where you are right now.
b. Construct a triad describing globalization.
c. Construct a triad describing what your body is doing as you consider this exercise.

C. PRESENT PERFECT

The present perfect tense is used to describe an action or existence that started in the past and has extended to the present. (I used the present perfect in this sentence: *has extended*.) It is also often used to express cumulative[20] experience. The words *recently, already, ever/never, lately, for/since*, and *yet* often signal that the present perfect tense should be used, as illustrated in the sentences below.

1. The police have already apprehended[21] a suspect, but they have not yet reported who the alleged perpetrator[22] is.
2. Although one political party has dominated Congress since 2014, recently, the other party has made significant gains.
3. Several excellent books on the topic of longevity have been published lately.

Exercise 1

Read the paragraph and answer the questions.

This course has already been offered for more than five years. Most students have found it to be quite helpful. Many have even come back to thank me for teaching them. I certainly have enjoyed teaching it and creating a textbook based on the lessons from this course, although a publisher for the book has not been found yet.

1. Where was the present perfect tense used?
2. Why was it chosen?

---

20 cumulative: adding up gradually
21 apprehended: arrested
22 perpetrator: a person who commits a crime

D. MIXED PRESENT TENSES

Consider the following paragraph and notice the various tenses and how they flow together.

> Professional football **has been** a major sport in the American sports scene for nearly a century, but many international students in the United States **do not understand** the game despite the attention that **is being paid** to it by Americans around them. Perhaps the international students **do not want** to learn about football because **the game does not exist** in their home countries. However, the National Football League (NFL) **is considering** expanding to include venues in Europe and perhaps in Asia. This desire by the NFL to expand overseas may result from the fact that viewership in the U.S. **has decreased** for the past two years.

1. What tense is each verb?
2. Why was each tense chosen?
3. Describe a sport in your country, including its history, current trends, and/or societal impact. You may find that you will need to use an occasional past tense as well.

E. SIMPLE PAST

The simple past tense can be used either to refer to

- an action or existence at a single point in the past
- a timespan that is completely in the past.

The second part is where many students struggle. Consider the following sentences, both of which are correct:

1. Many sources state that World War II began with the German invasion of Poland in 1939.
2. The world engaged in violent conflict from 1939 to 1945.

The major difficulty with the past tense is that there are many irregular verbs. The following list contains verbs that are often troublesome for students when they attempt to form the past tense. Fill in the empty cells in the table below with the simple past and the past participle. Write the past participle form with *has* to help you remember it.

Present	Past	Past Participle
allow		
benefit		
choose		
commit*		
confer*		
create		
die		

grow		
happen		
infer*		
learn		
lose		
occur*		
permit*		
prefer*		
raise		
rise		
run		
succeed		
teach		
travel		

The verbs with an asterisk (*) require special attention. Although they are regular verbs and take an –ed for the past tense and past participle, they require something else. What is it?

The final consonant must be doubled, right? But why is this so? When I ask this question, most students say something about consonant, vowel, consonant (CVC) for the last three letters, if they say anything at all. But if CVC is the reason, why aren't *happen, benefit,* and *travel* also asterisked? There is something else going on, and this is where proper pronunciation ties in with proper writing. The words that get the final consonant doubled have the CVC pattern, but they also have **stress on their final syllable!** The rule for American English is that if the last syllable is CVC **and it is stressed**, the final consonant must be doubled. *Allow* does not fit this pattern because its *w* is considered a glide, not a consonant.

One other common point of confusion is the overuse of the past perfect (*had* + past participle). Generally, the past perfect is used to distinguish an action or state in the past that occurred before some other action or state in the past. Consider the following sentence.

> 1. The perpetrator had already fled the scene when the police arrived.

In this sentence, the past perfect emphasizes that the fleeing occurred before the arrival of the police. However, this sentence can be paraphrased as follows:

> 2. The perpetrator fled the scene before the police arrived.

This sentence uses only the simple past because the adverb before explicitly states the time sequence. There is no need for the past perfect when a time adverb such as before or prior to is used.

> ✓ **Writing tip:** The past perfect truly is seldom used in academic writing. If you find yourself wanting to use it, be certain that it is necessary.

Exercise 1

Write a short paragraph on one of the following topics. You may want to describe how conditions were in the past, a change, and how conditions exist now. You'll need a variety of tenses. I will answer the third one as a model.

Model:

> The change in music over the past ten years can be exemplified in the music of Taylor Swift. Her songs ten years ago tended to be smooth, of a country style, and usually about love. The melodies were comfortable, clear, and catchy. However, in recent years, her songs have been about hatred (*Bad Blood*), and the melodies have all but disappeared. It seems like the lyrics of many pop songs are becoming increasingly critical of others and conceited, while melodies are becoming chaotic or even absent, and instrumental skill is now virtually unnecessary.

a. How has the use of technology developed over the past ten years?
b. How has your lifestyle changed in the last decade?
c. How has music changed in the past decade?
d. How have your techniques of studying English developed over the past decade?

Unit 4 Passive Voice

A. USING THE PASSIVE VOICE

There is a school of thought in composition writing that claims it is better to use the active voice than the passive voice. The idea is that the active voice is clearer, more energetic, and more captivating to the reader. However, the passive voice is, in fact, often used in academic writing, as it is essential to performing certain functions, including improving focus, communicating process, and omitting unknown or non-essential information.

At this point, it might be practical to consider sentence focus for a while. I learned an important lesson about sentence focus when I returned to the United States from Japan after living there for eight years. When speaking Japanese, the subject, which goes at the beginning of the sentence, is optional. That is, when the subject can easily be inferred from the situational context, it is omitted. The object and the verb come at the end of the sentence in Japanese, so when listening to Japanese, it is crucial to focus on the *end* of the sentence because that is where the main content is. When I returned to the U.S., for the first several days, I understood every word of what family and friends were saying to me, but in fact, most of what they were saying was going over my head. I had to ask for repetition, or I was often slow to process what they were saying. Why was this so? My brain was focusing on the *end* of sentences as I had become accustomed to doing in Japan, while the English speakers around me were putting their subjects and verbs at the *beginning* of their sentences, so I was missing the focus of what they were saying. It took several days for my brain to focus on the right part of sentences.

In writing, to focus on a certain word or phrase, authors move it to the front of the sentence. Consider the following examples:

1. In 1969, the first lunar[23] landing occurred.
2. The first lunar landing occurred in 1969.
3. Killer whales seldom attack great white sharks.
4. Seldom do killer whales attack great white sharks.

How do the sentences 1 and 2 differ? How do sentences 3 and 4 differ? They differ in focus, with the focus being at the front of the sentence.

It is clear that in general, the focus of English sentences is at the beginning of the sentence. Having established that principle, consider the following sentences.

5. People are buying more and more high-tech devices.
6. High-tech devices are being purchased at rising rates.
7. High-tech devices are growing in popularity.

What is the focus of the first sentence? *People*, right? Therefore, this sentence is stating the obvious because cows, dogs, or earthworms do not need technological devices.

---

23 lunar: related to the moon

Sentences 6 and 7 have the proper focus. Sentence 6 uses the passive voice, whereas sentence 7 uses an *intransitive* verb (*grow*).

Many students do not immediately understand what is meant by an **intransitive** verb or its opposite, a **transitive** verb. Understanding transitivity is essential to understanding the passive voice, so I will briefly explain this concept.

If I say, "Please do," does that make sense? It shouldn't. Your response should clearly be, "Do *what?*" *Do* is a transitive verb, and it makes no sense without an object such as *your homework* or *the dishes.*

A transitive verb requires an object.

On the other hand, if I said, "Please rise," it would make sense to you, and you would stand up. *Rise* does not require an object. It is an intransitive verb.

Intransitive verbs do not take objects.

Verbs can be transitive, intransitive, or both.

Understanding transitivity is essential to using the passive voice because **only transitive verbs can be made passive.** The passive is formed by taking the object of a transitive verb and making it the subject. **(Intransitive verbs cannot be made passive because they have no object.)** Then, the appropriate *be-* verb is inserted, and the transitive verb is changed to its past participle. The original subject becomes the agent, and may be placed after *by* after the verb if desired. Consider the example below:

<pre>
        S   V   O
1. John Booth assassinated[24] Lincoln. (Active with transitive verb)

   O→S be   p. part   (by +agent)
2. Lincoln was assassinated (by John Booth). (Passive)
</pre>

What is wonderful about the passive voice is that **the agent is optional.** Suppose the author did not know or care about *who* assassinated Lincoln, but was only pointing out the fact that Lincoln was shot to death while in office. The sentence *Lincoln was assassinated* is perfect. Presidents McKinley and Kennedy *were also assassinated*, and an assassination attempt *was made* on President Reagan as well. The passive voice perfectly fits this situation, and the agents can be omitted altogether.

---

24 assassinated: killed (often said of a political figure)

Exercise 1

Create passive sentences out of the following. (One sentence cannot be made passive.)

    a. Scientists are conducting vast amounts of research worldwide.
    b. Hackers stole the personal information of thousands of government employees.
    c. People produce billions of web pages each year.
    d. Children mature[25] physically faster now than they did 50 years ago.
    e. Adolescents commit more crime than they did 50 years ago.

The passive voice is also used to focus on processes. Now try Exercise 2.

Exercise 2

Underline the passive verbs in the following paragraph. Then answer the questions.

> The process of hearing is somewhat complicated. Sound waves are gathered by the outer ear so they strike the eardrum, which is caused to vibrate. These vibrations are amplified[26] by three bones in the middle ear. The amplified waves are then transmitted to the fluid-filled cochlea, where fluid waves are established. These waves ultimately cause hair cells in certain locations to be bent, leading to the firing of sensory neurons, sending auditory[27] information to the brain, where that information is interpreted.

    a. What passive verbs are used? Highlight them.
    b. When are agents specified? When are they not specified? Why?
    c. What is the purpose of this paragraph?
    d. What is the function of the passive voice in this paragraph?

Exercise 3

Write a paragraph in response to one of the following. Be sure to write in an academic tone and style that uses the passive voice. (Do not use *you, I, we,* or any of their forms, or the imperative.)

    a. How is rice cooked?
    b. How is food digested?
    c. How can a personal web page be constructed?

Another issue often arises with the passive voice. Certain verbs can be either transitive or intransitive, depending on the situation. *Change, open, increase,* and *decrease* are among the most common.

---

25 mature: grow up, become like an adult
26 amplified: make stronger and louder
27 auditory: related to hearing

Consider the following sentences.

> The weather changes frequently in the mountains.
> Because the weather changes so dramatically, mountain climbers may have to change their clothes.
> Due to severe weather, plans to climb the mountain changed.
> Due to severe weather, plans to climb the mountain were changed.

- In sentence 1, *change* is intransitive.
- In sentence 2, it is first intransitive, and then transitive.
- In sentence 3, it is intransitive.
- Sentence 4 is identical to Sentence 3 except that instead of an intransitive *change*, a passive voice transitive form of *change* is used.

Which sentence would be preferred, 3 or 4? Students often ask or are puzzled by this question. I would answer that simpler is better. I would therefore choose sentence 3. When the passive voice is used and the agent is omitted, a reader may wonder who the agent was and why it was omitted. (This critical reading process is sometimes called *reading between the lines*). Use of the passive voice invites reading between the lines, whereas the simple intransitive verb does not.

> ✓ **Writing tip:** When choosing between an intransitive verb and a passive transitive with no agent, choose the intransitive verb.

One more issue related to the passive voice are passive structures beginning with
> *It is _____ that ...*

These types of sentences are quite common in academic writing. Notice that this structure does not work with *consider*. Sentences like these improve the academic feel of a paper.

1. It is recommended that a slow transition from fossil fuels to renewable energy source be implemented.
2. It is suggested that intake of artificial sweeteners be reduced.
3. It was once believed that light was only a wave, but now it is known to have qualities of both waves and particles.
4. Light was once considered a wave, but now it is considered both a wave and a particle.

B. TRANSITIVITY

Below is a table of verbs with troublesome transitivity. Transitive verbs will **not** have a preposition immediately after them. If they did, the noun following the preposition would become the object of the preposition, and the transitive verb would lose its essential object.

Table 1: The transitivity of some important academic verbs.

Transitive	Intransitive
increase	increase
decrease	decrease
reduce	
decline (refuse)	decline (go down)
change	change
discuss	
contact	
lack	
consider	
impact	
influence	
improve	improve

Exercise 1

Mark whether the sentences below are correct or incorrect. If they are incorrect, determine why and decide how to fix them.

_____ a. Prices of vegetables were declined in May.

_____ b. The number of international students in the U.S. has increased each year since 2007.

_____ c. The policy on immigration was changed last month.

_____ d. The students discussed about how to divide labor for their group project.

_____ e. When the plug contacts with the outlet, electricity flows.

_____ f. The new policy will influence on everything from tuition to curriculum.

_____ g. It is considered important to reduce all types of waste

_____ h. The book was criticized because it lacked realism.

_____ i. Automobiles have been improved considerably in the past century.

_____ j. Each organism impacts many others, so the value of each one is incalculable[28].

---

28 incalculable: impossible to know the value of

Unit 5 Modal Verbs

A. GENERAL USE

The most common modal verbs in academic writing are shown in the table below.

can	could	
will	would	
	should	
may	might	must
have to*	had to	

But why are they called **modal verbs**? What does modal mean? A **mode** can be considered a function or a way of behaving. A smartphone has many modes: telephone, texting tool, Internet browser, alarm clock, scheduler, and more. A person has many modes. I may be a teacher, a parent, a husband, a coach, a player, and so on, and in each mode, I act a little differently. Modal verbs are similar; they have a variety of functions, and the challenge to the academic writer is to employ the functions clearly and skillfully.

The general syntax[29] of modal verbs is simple: they go before the verb they modify, the verb that follows them is in the plain, tense-less form, and they cannot be stacked (except for *have to,* which can follow other modal verbs, hence the asterisk in the table and the example in Sentence 4 below).

1. She will graduate next year.
2. He can run 100 meters in 10 seconds.
3. She should consult an advisor.
4. He might have to repeat the course if he keeps coming late to class.

Once more, there cannot be any tense attached to the main verb that follows a modal. If there is an adverb, its most natural placement is usually between the modal verb and the main verb.

5. She will probably graduate next year.
6. He can even run 100 meters in 10 seconds.
7. She should also consult with an advisor. (I used with in this sentence to demonstrate how either consult or consult with is acceptable.)
8. He might never have to take another English course if he passes this one.

Just for fun, compare the following sentences

9. Ken can even do this problem.
10. Even Ken can do this problem.

---

29 syntax: word order

What does each mean? How would you describe Ken in each sentence? Notice how important the placement of even can be.

Now, returning to the different modes that modals play, they may communicate possibility, probability, permission, reality/unreality, politeness/formality, time, or expectation. Here are some quick questions to clarify these modes.

1. Which is more polite, can or could?   (could)
2. Which is more probable, could or should?   (should)
3. Which is properly used to ask permission, may or can?   (may)
4. Which communicates a real possibility, can or could?
   (not considering politeness)   (can)
5. Which communicates an unreal possibility, will or would?   (would)
6. Which communicates past time, had to or must?   (had to)
7. Which implies stronger expectation, should or has to?   (has to)

Skillful use of modals involves using modals unambiguously. Notice in item 4 above, I had to say "not considering politeness" because *could*, in fact, can be used to politely communicate real possibility.

8. If you would like, you could try the lobster.

This sense is not so common in academic writing, though. However, *could* is often mistakenly used ambiguously to communicate ability in the past.

9. When I was young, I could play tennis. (Does this mean I was able to play tennis, or that I was allowed to play tennis?)

> ✓ **Writing tip:** Use *was able* to or *will be able to* instead of *could* or *can* to communicate ability in the past or future clearly.

Perhaps the most serious errors related to modals are in communicating real or unreal (hypothetical) situations. Suppose one is writing about space exploration and the establishment of colonies on Mars or some other planet.

Paragraph 1

If a colony[30] on Mars were to be established, it would have to include facilities to produce water. It would also have to create greenhouses for growing food, and these greenhouses would need to be insulated[31] well enough to protect the plants from brutally cold Martian temperatures.

---

a. What is the tone here? Is it hypothetical[32] or realistic? How do you know?
b. Compare it with the following.

---

30 colony: a small group trying to settle a new place
31 insulated: designed to trap heat
32 hypothetical: imaginary

Paragraph 2

If a colony on Mars is established, it will have to include facilities to produce water. It will also have to create greenhouses for growing food, and these greenhouses will need to be insulated well enough to protect the plants from brutally cold Martian temperatures.

    c. What is the tone here? How do you know?
    d. Now consider the following.

Paragraph 2

If a colony on Mars is established, it would have to include facilities to produce water. It will also have to create greenhouses for growing food, and these greenhouses would need to be insulated well enough to protect the plants from brutally cold Martian temperatures. X

    e. What's the tone here? Do you see what's wrong? Do you understand how confusing this paragraph is to the reader?

✓ **Writing tip:** Once a realistic or hypothetical tone is established, every subsequent verb within the situational framework must be consistently marked to maintain that tone; otherwise, confusion results.

Exercise 1

Choose one of the following questions and write a paragraph response.

    a. What can be done to make cars safer?
    b. What could be done to make cars safer if there were no budgetary limits?

Exercise 2

Answer the following prompt. Provide reasons in your response.

What should be done by a traveler preparing for a trip to your home city?

B. HEDGING

Modal verbs are also often used in academic writing to **hedge** statements; that is, to soften them to protect them from criticism and to avoid overstating an opinion. Consider the following sentence.

1. Global warming is the most serious crisis facing the world today.

Do you agree with this statement? Can you think of other possible issues that might be more serious? (Perhaps poverty, nuclear war, or ideological[33] conflict?) How could this sentence be hedged to prevent a critical reaction from the reader?

2. Global warming may be the most serious crisis facing the world today.

(*Might*, *could*, or *is* arguably could also be used.)

Exercise 3

Write properly hedged sentences on the following themes.

a. Trump, most controversial American president
b. Boxing, most hazardous[34] sport
c. Education, number one priority for government
d. Snow tomorrow
e. Dinosaur extinction, meteor[35]
f. Printing press, most significant invention
g. Cats, better pets than dogs, because …

---

33 ideological: related to political/religious ideas
34 hazardous: dangerous/risky
35 meteor: a large space rock that falls from the sky

Unit 6 Nouns

Nouns in English are complicated. Associated with nouns are the concept of countability, quantifiers that are determined by countability, articles that also depend on countability, adjectival uses of nouns, and nominalization (the process of converting other parts of speech to nouns for concise expression of concepts).

A. CAPITALIZATION

Even before countability, nouns can be classified as **proper** (like China, Edison, or Math 112), which are capitalized, and **common**, which are not. Advanced students don't tend to struggle with capitalization except except in the same ways Americans do: course names, position titles, and titles in general.

Quick tips on capitalization:

1. Course names are capitalized, but subjects are not (unless they are already proper nouns such as nation or language names).

   a. Her major is chemistry, so she is required to take Chemistry 400.
   b. International Relations 630 is the highest course offered for those who study international relations.
   c. All Italian majors must take Italian 550 and study abroad in Italy.

2. Position titles are not usually capitalized unless they are followed by names.

   a. Many people were surprised that President Washington did not wish to remain president for more than two terms.

3. For titles of written works, major words (not articles or prepositions, unless they are the first word or the first word after a colon) are capitalized. (Rules vary in reference lists.)

   a. *The Cat in the Hat*
   b. *Grammar Choices for Graduate and Professional Writers*
   c. *2001: A Space Odyssey*

4. When writing by hand, make sure the **C** in **C**hina is as high as the backbone of the **h**, and that the **A** of **A**rabia is as high as the backbone of the **b**. Otherwise, they will appear uncapitalized.

B. COUNTABILITY

Countability is not necessarily intuitive. Money is not countable even though people count it regularly, while stars are countable even though no one can count them. Some words are even countable sometimes and not countable at other times. Thus, reading and listening to standard English are important, and attention must be paid to the countability of nouns.

Exercise 1

Look back at the previous paragraph and highlight countable(c) nouns with one color and non-count (nc) nouns with another color.

    a. Did you notice that nouns with a plural –s are countable?
    b. Did you notice that concept words and gerunds are not countable?
    c. Is time always countable, as it was here?
    d. Money is not countable; so when people count money, what are they actually counting?

Exercise 2

Answer the following questions.

    a. Where would you buy hamburger (nc)? Where would you buy a hamburger (c)?
    b. Where would you buy a water? How do you get water?
    c. What is meant by technology? Why do some schools teach technologies? (hint: kinds)

The number of nouns in English is countless, so a book of practical grammar cannot deal with them all. However, here are some non-count nouns that advanced students often make mistakes with, along with countable words of similar meanings.

Table 2: Commonly mistaken non-count nouns with their countable synonyms

Non-Count	Count
research	study, investigation, survey, questionnaire
homework	assignments
advice	suggestion, tip
technology	technique
knowledge	fact, concept, idea
information	fact
evidence	clue

Exercise 3

Correct the following sentences. Two are already correct.

    a. Many researches have shown that a vitamin A deficiency[36] causes blindness.
    b. The police could not find any evidence that suggested that the victim knew his assailant[37].
    c. The course was beneficial because students gained many knowledges.

---

36 deficiency: lack
37 assailant: an attacker

d. A large-scale investigation was conducted to discover the psychological factors associated with longevity.
e. That course is difficult because of all the homeworks.
f. The counselor offered the students many advices.
g. Informations are easy to access on the Internet.

C. QUANTIFIERS

In speech, especially informal and non-academic speech, quantifiers are not difficult because *a lot* can be used universally, whether the noun is countable or not. The problem comes in academic writing, where *a lot* is inappropriate because of its informality. Thus, more academically appropriate quantifiers should be chosen, but this can be tricky. Some quantifiers are used with countable nouns, and others are used with non-count nouns. **Table 3** displays a variety of academic quantifiers and the type of nouns they accompany.

Table 3: **Academic non-count and count quantifiers**

Non-Count	Count
much* (acceptable, but low-level vocabulary)	many* (acceptable, but low-level vocabulary)
a large/great/small/considerable amount of	numerous
a significant/an insignificant amount of	countless
	innumerable
a large/great/small/considerable volume of	several
a significant/an insignificant volume of	a multitude of
	a plethora of
a large/small/significant/an insignificant quantity of	a large/small/significant/an insignificant number of

✓ **Writing tip:** *Many* and *much* are common in academic writing, but they do not display a high level of vocabulary. In a situation where an academic impression is desirable, other quantifiers should be chosen.

Exercise 1

What quantifier would you choose with the following nouns to display a high level of vocabulary? Write a sentence with each word.

h. research
i. oxygen
j. information
k. furniture
l. money

m. studies
n. evidence
o. gasoline
p. concepts
q. complexity

D. ARTICLES

When asked what the purpose of language is, most will immediately answer, "To communicate." However, linguists have identified a variety of purposes of language, including "to distinguish the in-group from the out-group." What they mean by this expression is that every language seems to have certain features that are so difficult that the only way to use them well is to be a native speaker (the in-group). Those who can perform those difficult features only poorly are easily identified as the out-group. In English, the use of articles seems to be one of those difficult features. Nevertheless, certain aspects of the article system can be learned and mastered to a high degree, resulting in language similar enough to native English for the non-native writer to be welcomed into the academic community.

Here are some easy rules:

- *the* always comes before *same*

- *a* is associated with *similar*

- *the* comes before ordinal adjectives such as *first, second, tenth, next, last,* and *final*

- *the* comes before common countable nouns of which only one exists or is significant, such as *the sun, the moon,* or *the environment* (meaning the big global environment)

- *a* is used to introduce a countable noun, but subsequently, *the* is used.

- superlative adjectives (*–est, most + adj.*) require *the.*

Other concepts related to articles are more difficult. They are related to countability. Here are some other basic rules:

- Non-count nouns usually need no article.

- Count nouns need an article (or other determiner) if they are singular. (Think of count nouns as being lonely, so they either go in groups – plural, or with a companion – an article or a determiner.)

- Plural count nouns usually do not require an article.

- Any noun that is specified clearly will take *the.*

Exercise 1

Apply the rules above to fill in the blanks in the following true story of Manjiro Nakahama.
(Ø for no article is also an option.)

¹_____ 14-year-old fatherless Japanese boy born in ²_____ early 1800s went on to influence ³_____ history significantly. One day, ⁴_____ boy and several of his friends went fishing. They were blown by ⁵_____ storm to ⁶_____ island far from Japan. ⁷_____ storm wrecked their boat, so they stayed on ⁸_____ island several months eating⁹_____ crabs, ¹⁰_____fish, and ¹¹_____ occasional albatross (a large bird). One day ¹²_____ whaling ship from ¹³_____ United States discovered ¹⁴_____ boys

on ^{15}_____ island because ^{16}_____ cook on ^{17}_____ ship wanted to find ^{18}_____ turtles for ^{19}_____ turtle soup. ^{20}_____ boys were taken to ^{21}_____ ship, and ^{22}_____ 14-year-old eventually reached ^{23}_____ Massachusetts, where he was adopted and educated. Eventually, he returned to ^{24}_____ Japanese Islands and influenced ^{25}_____ political leaders there to sign ^{26}_____ treaty of ^{27}_____ peace and ^{28}_____ trade with ^{29}_____ U. S. This treaty began ^{30}_____ industrialization of ^{31}_____ Japan, which began ^{32}_____ modernization of ^{33}_____ Asia. ^{34}_____ boy became one of ^{35}_____ most influential Japanese men in ^{36}_____ history of Japan.

Generally speaking, proper nouns do not require articles. Nevertheless, if their names contain specification by adjective or *of*-phrase, they will require *the*. It is always the same rule: clear specification requires *the* regardless of the type of noun.

Exercise 2

Which proper nouns will take *the?* Why?

a. _____ England	b. _____ China(	
c. _____ Saudi Arabia	d. _____ United States	
e. _____ Walmart	f. _____ People's Republic of China	
g. _____ Commonwealth of Virginia	h. _____ City of Philadelphia	
i. _____ Maine	j. _____ Kingdom of Saudi Arabia	
k. _____ Delaware River	l. _____ Rockies	
m. _____ France	n. _____ Aleutian Islands	
o. _____ Aleutians		

Exercise 3

Answer (discuss) the following questions.

a. In a significant event in American history, George Washington crossed the Delaware. What exactly did he cross?

b. What creatures inhabit Mississippi? What creatures inhabit the Mississippi?

E. ADJECTIVAL NOUNS

Nouns can be used like adjectives to modify other nouns. They are usually used when there is no adjective form for the adjectival noun. For example, there is no adjective form for *computer*. This adjectival use of nouns allows for stacking of nouns, and it is often used in academic writing to condense meaning and make sentences more efficient. Consider the following sentences.

1. Office computer size specifications are required. (6 words)
2. Specifications for the sizes of computers for offices are required. (10 words)

Did you notice how the nouns in Sentence 1 are stacked, resulting in a 40% more efficient sentence than Sentence 2? This efficiency is especially important in writing abstracts, cover letters, or articles for publications where the number of words is often limited.

One feature to notice about adjectival nouns is that they are not plural.

Another helpful feature of adjectival nouns is that they can be used to eliminate awkward[38] apostrophes ('). Consider the following sentences.

3. The office's computer's monitor is malfunctioning.
4. The office computer monitor is malfunctioning.

Which would you consider more academic? If you chose Sentence 4, you are correct. Apostrophes are awkward both to write and to read, so academic writers tend to avoid them.

Occasionally adjectival nouns are hyphenated. For example, a break that lasts ten days would be a *ten-day break*. Notice again that there is no *–s* on *ten-day*. In English, adjectives do not get an *-s* to make them plural. (Some other languages do add an *–s* to adjectives of plural nouns.)

Exercise 1

Condense the following sentences using adjectival nouns.
   a. The stereo for the car is in the shop for repairs.
   b. There is a break for two weeks over the holidays.
   c. The presentations that students make are 30 minutes long along with a period for questions and answers that lasts 15 minutes.
   d. The laws for driving occasionally differ between states.

Sometimes a choice has to be made between an adjectival noun and a true adjective. For example, would it be better to write *president election* or *presidential election*? **In general, if the true adjective exists, use it**. However, sometimes there is a difference in meaning. A *health problem* is different from a *healthy problem*. Can you tell the difference?

A *health problem* is a problem related to health, whereas a *healthy problem* is oxymoronic (seemingly opposite words next to each other), and does not make much sense.

---

38 awkward: poorly balanced, strange

Exercise 2

Choose the correct word.

    a. I read an (education/educational) book.
    b. This paper analyzes the (education/educational) system of Spain.
    c. The student is writing an (economics/economic/economical) paper. (hint: Economics ends with an s, but it is not plural)
    d. This (relaxation/relaxing) article teaches several methods to reduce stress and improve rest.
    e. (Geography/geographical) textbooks explain many (geography/geographical) features.
    f. Runners should wear (reflective/reflection) clothes at night.
    g. No one ever fails this course, so it is a (safe/safety) class to take.
    h. Children should take (safe/safety) courses in elementary school.
    i. (Science/scientific) discoveries have transformed society.
    j. (Science/scientific) textbooks need updating frequently.

Exercise 3

It is time to write. Choose one of the topics below and write a paragraph, focusing on your use of nouns, articles, quantifiers, and adjectival nouns. Remember that plurals are used for writing generalities related to count nouns, and singular nouns require the 3rd person singular present –s/-es.

    a. What do universities contribute to society?
    b. How has technology affected food?

Exercise 4

One more challenging final exercise on nouns. What is wrong with the following sentences? ("Nothing" is a possibility.)

    1. The society needs laborers with a high level of education.
    2. The police is coming to gather information about the crime.
    3. If lessons can be learned from the history, civilization can advance.
    4. The history of the U.S. is not nearly as long as that of China.
    5. The nature is the greatest inspiration for engineers.
    6. The life is full of irony.
    7. The life of O. Henry, the American short story writer, was difficult and tragic.
    8. Government is a necessary evil: without it, there is chaos; but with it, there are restrictions on freedom.
    9. American government consists of three branches.
    10. An economy based on consumption can be dangerous to environment.

F. NOMINALIZATION

As previous explained in the Focus section, nominalization is often useful to maintain focus. It is also useful for cohesion, paraphrasing, parallel structure, and efficiency. However, nominalization is tricky because there are numerous ways to create nouns from verbs, either by making them gerunds or ordinary nouns; adjectives; or other nouns; and the way is particular to each word. Nevertheless, there are certain patterns, which will become apparent with some work.

Below are some words that appear in first-year academic textbooks (biology, political science, rhetoric, and sociology) that can be nominalized. Challenge yourself to fill in the noun columns. Answers are in the back of the book.

Verb	Noun	Verb	Noun
accept		cover	
accuse		criticize	
acknowledge		debate	
affirm		decide	
aggregate		declare	
amend		defame	
analyze		defend	
annoy		define	
appeal		demonstrate	
apply		denature	
approach		depress	
approve		derive	
argue		derive	
assemble		describe	
associate		deter	
attempt		determine	
behave		develop	
benefit		disagree	
bond		discriminate	
bribe		discuss	
cite		disenfranchise	
claim		dissent	
coincide		distract	
commit		embezzle	
communicate		emerge	
compare		emphasize	
compensate		equivocate	
compete		establish	
compose		execute	
conceive		exhibit	

concentrate		explain	
condense		expose	
conduct		express	
conflict		extend	
confuse		flatter	
constitute		frustrate	
control		generalize	
convict		generate	
cooperate		grow	
court		hinder	
hydrolyze		protest	
implement		provide	
impress		provoke	
imprison		publish	
incite		punish	
inform		react	
injure		recommend	
institutionalize		recruit	
insulate		rehabilitate	
interfere		reinforce	
internalize		release	
invest		represent	
justify		reproduce	
label		reserve	
legislate		resist	
manipulate		restrain	
metabolize		restrict	
modify		revolve	
notify		rob	
observe		sanction	
offend		saturate	
oppose		seduce	
oppose		socialize	
organize		state	
participate		stigmatize	
perceive		store	
persevere		substitute	
persist		suggest	
persuade		support	
pity		suppress	
plagiarize		tend	

possess		transport	
present		treat	
preside		utter	
promote		value	
protect		vary	

Adjective	Noun	Adjective	Noun
abundant		homosexual	
acceptable		hyperactive	
accessible		ideal	
acidic		important	
active		inconvenient	
addictive		independent	
adolescent		inevitable	
alcoholic		interior	
analogous		intimate	
bureaucratic		just	
causal		lazy	
cognitive		major	
complex		malicious	
confident		moral	
consistent		necessary	
controversial		normless	
corrupt		nutritious	
credible		obscene	
criminal		polar	
delinquent		poor	
democratic		probable	
depraved		prominent	
deviant		rational	
difficult		residential	
diverse		responsible	
easy		safe	
effective		scholarly	
eloquent		strong	
emotional		sympathetic	
equal		true	
evil		violent	
false		vulgar	
free		wicked	
frequent			

What patterns do you see?

What exceptions do you see?

Below are the same words grouped by the noun endings they have in common.

Nominalization of verbs

-sis	-ment	-sion/ion	-tion/ion	-ation	-ition	**-tion	(none)
*emphasize	argue	persuade	communicate	present	oppose	conceive	benefit
hydrolyze	disagree	depress	equivocate	cite	compete	perceive	approach
analyze	develop	discuss	convict	observe	compose	provoke	convict
	reinforce	express	cooperate	generalize	define	describe	appeal
	amend	provide	distract	recommend			pity
	recruit	extend	demonstrate	determine			aggregate
	state	confuse	substitute	inform			bond
	acknow-ledge	possess	react	accuse			claim
		impress	insulate	implement			conflict
-ence	punish		saturate	represent		**-y**	recruit
coincide	commit		reproduce	condense		flatter	dissent
persevere	treat		concentrate	derive		assemble	support
transcend	invest		Constitute	transport		injure	conduct
emerge	disen-franchise		dissent	denature			protest
interfere			conduct	*vary	**-ism**		value
persist	embezzle		compensate	*publish	plagiarize		debate
*deter			restrict	affirm	metabolize		release
	-ance		participate	declare	criticize		sanction
	resist		discriminate	*apply			attempt
	*hinder		suggest	defame			label
	annoy		frustrate	organize			
-ent	**-ant**	** -se	exhibit	*explain			
preside	defend	defend	seduce	reserve			
		offend	promote	stigmatize			
			manipulate	institution-alize	**Bizarre N forms**		
-ency	**-t**	**-age**	generate		concept	**-ication**	
tend	restrain	store	rehabilitate		behavior	justify	
emerge	constrain	cover	execute		approval	notify	
			internalize		exposure	modify	
			associate		growth		
-ship	**-ry/-ery**		legislate		comparison		
court	*rob						
	bribe						

Nominalization of adjectives

-ity	-ization	-ce	-ness	**-y	Bizarre N
rational	rational	confident	effective	sympathetic	falsehood
emotional		independent	scholarly	bureaucratic	fallacy
moral		abundant	lazy	democratic	truth
polar		*residential	normless	safe	analogy
acidic*		eloquent	wicked	difficult	justice
equal		violent		controversial	strength
major		inconvenient		intimate	ease
vulgar		prominent			freedom
obscene		deviant			malice
necessary*		important			poverty
homosexual		adolescent		**-cy**	
criminal				delinquent	
hyperactive	**-ion**			frequent	
causal	nutritious			consistent	
depraved	cognitive				
active	addictive				
complex	corrupt				
diverse					
				No change	
				ideal	
-ility		**-ism**		interior	
acceptable		ideal		deviant	
credible		alcoholic		alcoholic	
accessible				evil	
probable					
responsible					
inevitable					

It is probably very clear that using nominalized forms of words reveals highly developed vocabulary and word-level grammar; thus, nominalization is a clear sign of university-level writing. Now that the complexity of how to nominalize is understood, we can approach the practical purposes of nominalization.

1. Nominalization aids cohesion. Nominalized forms can be used to refer back to previous statements, as demonstrated below.

   a. The CEO *stated* that the company was going *bankrupt*[39]. **This** underlined statement caught stockholders by surprise, and there was much concern about how to deal with the forthcoming bankruptcy.

Notice how the underlined words refer back to the italicized words, creating strong cohesion. Especially

---

39 bankrupt: not having enough funds to pay bills

notice the word <u>statement</u>, which follows the bolded **This.** Was the word <u>statement</u> necessary? Honestly speaking, many writers would omit <u>statement</u> (resulting in what I call a *naked this*) because it is not so necessary in spoken English. However, in writing, including the word <u>statement</u> increases clarity and improves cohesion.

> ✓ **Writing tip:** When using a demonstrative (*this, that, these, those*) to refer to previous information, add a noun after it for clarity and cohesion. The noun should answer the question "This WHAT?" If a specific nominalized word does not come to mind, general words like *idea, concept, notion, process, development*, or *event* can help to avoid the "naked *this*."

Exercise 1

Fill in the blanks in the sentences below to refer back to the first sentence provided.

a. An Arkansas woman was executed[40] last night. This _____ was the first in the nation in 2018.

b. A new tax law was passed in Congress yesterday. This _____ will be a major overhaul[41] of the tax system.

c. Title IX states that women and men should be able to access sports in school equally. This _____ has not yet been accomplished, as women have limited _____ to football, and men have limited _____ to volleyball.

d. Water is abundant in tropical rainforests. This _____ of water leads to massive amounts of vegetation and huge animal populations.

e. Lincoln was not a handsome man, but he was an eloquent[42] speaker. This _____ is noticeable in his Gettysburg Address.

f. Employers must compensate workers who are injured on the job. This _____ usually consists of paying for hospitalization, rehabilitation, and lost work time.

g. See how many examples of nominalization you can find in sentences d and f.

2. Nominalization is also useful in paraphrasing. Consider the following passage and its paraphrase.

a. Plants can photosynthesize glucose from carbon dioxide and water in an elaborate chemical process that involves many enzymes[43].

b. *Photosynthesis* creates glucose from water and carbon dioxide through a series of complex enzymatic reactions.

Notice the italicized nominalizations in Sentence b. Also notice the shift in focus from *plants* in Sentence a to *photosynthesis* in Sentence b.

---

40 executed: killed by government for a crime
41 overhaul: a change that affects ever aspect
42 eloquent: having sophisticated speech
43 enzymes: special proteins that speed up reactions

Exercise 2

Paraphrase the following short passages employing nominalization.

   a. As the global atmosphere warms, deserts will probably expand, and many plant and animal species will likely go extinct.
   b. When companies seek to globalize, they often shift operations that manufacture goods to nations where the price of labor is lower.

1. Nominalization also aids in summarizing and improves efficiency because it can express complex ideas in one term. Consider the following two passages.

   a. Writing by hand has changed incredibly over the centuries. Long ago, feathers were dipped in ink to write. After that, fountain pens were invented, but they were difficult to carry. Finally, ball point pens were created, enabling pens to be carried and used anywhere. (45 words)
   b. The evolution of writing instruments includes transitions from feathers to fountain pens to ball-point pens. Each transition facilitated writing and the transportation of writing tools. (26 words)

Notice the efficiency of the Sentence b compared to Sentence a and the nominalized forms that were employed.

Exercise 3

Paraphrase and summarize the following passage to make it more efficient.

   In the early days of American society, villages were small, and the economy was mostly agricultural. Churches were often at the centers of communities, so those churches contributed greatly to controlling the behavior of the citizens of those villages. However, as America became more urban and industrial, society also became more complex, and public education, courts, and prisons became the major factors in regulating social conduct (Kornblum, 2008).

Unit 7 Prepositions

What are prepositions, anyway? Looking within the word *preposition, pre-* means "before" and *pos* means "put," so a preposition is a word that is put before something. That "*something*" is a noun. The noun that comes after a preposition is called the object of the preposition.

Most students who have reached the advanced level agree that English prepositions are difficult. Most ESL teachers concur. To be honest, most of the time, even if an error with a preposition occurs, it does not usually interfere with comprehensibility, so little attention tends to be paid to prepositions. However, prepositions are very common, and sloppy use of prepositions results in a generally sloppy impression, so a little focus on prepositions is necessary.

One serious grammatical problem arises when prepositions are used as verbs, as in the following erroneous sentences.

1. The public against the new parking regulations.   X
2. After graduating from American universities, most international students back to their home country.   X

Against and *back* are prepositions and cannot be used as verbs. How would you correct Sentences 1 and 2 above? (Hint: *be, go, oppose, return*)

Perhaps the most important role of prepositions in advanced writing is their collocative use; that is, certain prepositions go with certain other words. Some common examples include:

> pay attention *to* (not *on*)
> consist *of*
> invest *in*
> a reason *for* (not *of*)
> insist *on*

But is there any rule that governs the collocation[44] system or any pattern that students can learn to help them choose what preposition to use with academic vocabulary they are learning? It turns out that there is.

A. VERB + PREPOSITION COLLOCATIONS

Generally speaking, the preposition that follows a verb with a prefix is consistent with the meaning of the prefix.

I. The Latin prefixes *ad-*, *at-*, *ap-* mean "to."

Applying the general rule, complete the following sentences:

1. He intends to apply _____ the University of Delaware.

---

44 collocation: words that usually occur together

2. International students need to adjust _____ the culture of their host country.
3. The file is attached _____ the email she sent.
4. Humans can adapt _____ a variety of climates.
5. She adheres[45] _____ a strict diet and exercise regimen.
6. She was admitted _____ the University of Delaware.
7. This new document should be appended _____ the existing one.
8. She cannot attend the meeting because she has to attend _____ more urgent matters.
9. His success can be attributed _____ his fitness regimen.

II. The Latin prefixes *co-*, *con-*, and *com-* mean "with."

Applying the general rule, complete the following sentences:

1. The suspect cooperated _____ the police.
2. Skype makes it easier for university students to communicate _____ their parents.
3. That event coincided _____ the full moon.
4. This company competes _____ the other company. (against could also be used)
5. The doctor will confer _____ her patient.
6. The CEO will consult _____ several advisors.
7. The meeting will be commenced _____ a moment of silence to commemorate[46] the deceased.
8. The symphony will conclude _____ a loud clash of cymbals.
9. Her story greatly contrasts _____ his.
10. The time of the concert conflicts _____ their schedules.
11. The goal is to coordinate our activities _____ those of the students on the other campus.
12. The witness saw the defendant conversing _____ the victim on the night of the crime.
13. The new product complies _____ new safety regulations.

Some notable exceptions: *con-* → "of"

 a. The cake consists mostly _____ flour and milk.
 b. She could hardly conceive[47] _____ her husband's leaving her.

Other exceptions: *con-* → "to"

 c. The child was confined _____ his room.
 d. Her behavior does not conform _____ the expectations of her parents.
   (*to* is about 10 times more common than *with*)

_____

45 adhere: stick to, follow
46 commemorate: show respect to a historical figure or event
47 conceive: imagine

    e. Compared _____ last year, this year had much more snow.
       (*to* is about 1.5 times more common than *with*)
    f. Her efforts contributed greatly _____ the success of the team.
       (*Contribute* means "give.")

III. The Latin prefixes *ab-*, *dis-*, e-, *ex-*, and *se-* are related to "from."

Applying the general rule, fill in the following sentences:

1. Three senators abstained[48] _____ voting.
2. It is difficult to distinguish alligators _____ crocodiles.
3. The first step in the process is to separate solids _____ liquids.
4. South Carolina seceded[49] _____ the Union in 1860.
5. The soccer match distracted students _____ their studies.
6. That politician emerged _____ obscurity[50] around the age of 30.
7. The team lost, so it was eliminated _____ the tournament.
8. The ruling party believed that such ideas must be eradicated[51] _____ the population.
9. The hermit chose to seclude himself _____ society.
10. Her results differ _____ his.
11. He was excluded _____ the club because he was not from that neighborhood.
12. This passage was extracted _____ a 200-page book.
13. Waste products are excreted _____ cells into the bloodstream and filtered out by the kidneys.

Notable exceptions: *dis-/ex-* → "to"

    a. If plants are exposed _____ light, they can make sugar through photosynthesis.
    b. The Great Plains extend _____* the Rocky Mountains _____ the Mississippi River. *(not *to*)
    c. Copies of the file were distributed _____ all parties involved with the project.

IV. Miscellaneous:

Pay attention **to** (related to the *at-* prefix of *attention*)

    It is difficult to pass a test without *paying attention to* the instructions.

Prevent/Prohibit/Restrain _____ **from:**

    Being a woman did not prevent Curie _____ becoming a great scientist.

    The new rule prohibits students _____ parking in that area.

---

48 abstained: refused
49 secede: pull away from, separate from
50 obscurity: the state of being unknown
51 eradicated: completely removed

Persuade/Convince/Challenge someone **to** do something (infinitive)

The speaker challenged his listeners _____ change the world by voting for his brother, and although he persuaded most _____ vote the following day, he was unable to convince many _____ back his brother.

Insist **on** doing something:

She insists _____ coming to class late even though her grades are dropping.

Persist **in** doing something:

He developed his vocabulary by persisting _____ reading extensively.

Object **to:**

The lawyer objected _____ her client's being questioned in that particular manner.

Result **from** (a cause); Result **in** (an effect)

The swelling resulted _____ an infection. If untreated, the infection could result _____ death.

TEST YOURSELF

1. By attending carefully _____ her own duties, she gained a promotion.

2. Contrasting photo A _____ photo B, it is clear that the suitcase was moved.

3. By always insisting _____ her own way, she lost many friends.

4. The ants emerged _____ their anthill and started scavenging for food.

5. After having been diagnosed with a liver problem, the patient had to abstain _____ drinking alcohol.

6, 7. Cell phones distract drivers __ _ paying attention _____ the road.

8, 9. The children were excluded _____ their parents' conversation in order to prevent the children _____ becoming excessively worried.

10, 11. If babies are exposed _____ cigarette smoke at an early age, it could result _____ their developing asthma.

12, 13. If teenagers eliminated obscene language _____ their speaking, they could probably communicate more deeply _____ their parents.

14, 15. The suspect objected _____ being confined _____ a prison cell while awaiting trial.

16. This exercise consists _____ reading sentences and filling blanks with prepositions.

17, 18. He could not persuade her _____ (two words) what he wanted because her opinions differed greatly _____ his.

19, 20. The student was dismissed because he could not adapt _____ the new academic environment or conform _____ the expectations of his professors.

The following verbs are transitive and do not take any preposition, although their noun forms do:

    contact, impact, influence, lack

The noun *contact* is associated with *with*, as would be expected (*con-* → *with*).
The nouns *impact* and *influence* are associated with *on*.
The noun *lack* requires *of*.

1. She promised to contact _____ him after she arrived in England.
2. The new policy will greatly impact _____ economic development.
3. The teacher influenced _____ many children positively over the course of her career.
4. The course lacks _____ instructors to teach it, so it will not be offered.
5. The delinquent[52] father was instructed by the court to have no contact _____ his children.
6. Diet exerts a tremendous impact _____ long-term health.
7. It is difficult to predict the influence the new law will have _____ unemployment.
8. The proposal was rejected because of the lack _____ a specific time frame.

---

52 delinquent: irresponsible

Unit 8 Gerunds and Infinitives

Gerunds and infinitives are verbal expressions that fulfill roles that are different from ordinary verbs. A gerund, for example, is a **verb + ing**, and it functions as a noun, while preserving verb characteristics such as transitivity. Consider the following sentence.

1. Cleaning glassware properly is essential to effective research in chemistry.

Notice how *Cleaning* is the subject of the sentence, but it also keeps it verb-like trait of taking an object (*glassware*). Gerunds can play any function in a sentence that nouns can play: they can be subjects, complements, objects of verbs, or objects of prepositions. Consider what roles gerunds play in the following sentences.

2. Doctors do not endorse smoking.
3. By saving money regularly, it may be possible to retire early.

In Sentence 2, *smoking* is a direct object. In Sentence 3, *saving* is the object of the preposition *by*.

Infinitives are *to* + plain verb, and they can function as nouns (answering the question *what*), adverbs (answering the question *why* or *how*), or adjectives (answering the question *what kind of*). No matter what role they play, they maintain transitivity. Consider the roles played by the infinitives in the following sentences.

4. To become a better person was the most common New Year's resolution for 2018.
5. Seeking to improve character seems to have replaced seeking physical fitness as the most common goal. (There are two infinitives here.)
6. Unfortunately, to improve character, facing adversity is often necessary.
7. It is questionable whether those seeking character improvement have the courage to welcome adversity.

In Sentence 4, *to become* is a _____ , and it is the _____ of the sentence.

In Sentence 5, *to improve* is a _____, and it is the _____.

In Sentence 6, *to improve* is a(n) _____.

In sentence 7, *to welcome* functions as a(n) _____.

A. CAUSATIVES AND INFINITIVES

Causative expressions communicate that **X causes Y to happen**. The most common causative expressions involve *let* and *make*, but neither of these words is very academic, so writers are usually encouraged to choose more sophisticated ways to communicate causation. However, it is still essential to distinguish between *let* and *make*. Consider the following sentences.

8. The teacher let the students stay late.
9. The teacher made the students stay late.

What's the difference in meaning? The key is the volition of the students. In Sentence 8, the students want to stay, but in Sentence 9, they do NOT want to stay late.

Once that difference is clear, a table can be created with academic expressions for *let* and *make*, and also for another category that I will label *help*. The ... in each place is the noun that does the action.

Table 4: Academic causative expressions

Let ... ~~to~~ Verb	Make ... ~~to~~ Verb	Help ...(to) Verb
allow ... to Verb	cause ... to Verb	assist ... to
permit ... to Verb	command ... to Verb	enable ... to
	compel ... to Verb	encourage ... to
	force ... to Verb	inspire ... to
	lead ... to	
	order ... to Verb	
	require ... to Verb	

What pattern exists? Every academic causative expression includes *to*: that is, **they all require infinitives**.

What happened to *let, make,* and *help*? It is a little like texting, where the most common expressions become abbreviated. As language evolves, the most common expressions tend to become simplified, but less common (more academic) expressions maintain the standard, traditional pattern. *Help* seems to be in the process of evolving, as it will work with or without *to*.

> ✓ **Writing tip:** Do not forget the *to* in academic causative expressions.

B. PURPOSE PHRASES

Another common use for infinitives is to communicate purpose, as in the following structure.

    1. The goal/purpose/aim/objective/desire of this X is to Y.

X will be a noun such as *book, experiment,* or *program*, and Y will be a verb to complete the infinitive.

Exercise 1

Complete the following sentences with causative or purpose expressions.

    a. The new policy will force _____.
    b. The instructor permitted _____.
    c. The surgery will enable _____.
    d. The captain led _____.
    e. Her parents inspired _____.
    f. The purpose of this exercise is _____.
    g. The goal of this course is _____.
    h. The aim of the coach was ___ encourage his team _____.
    i. Global warming may cause the ice caps _____, which could lead to higher sea levels, which could compel coastal dwellers _____.

C. GERUND OR INFINITIVE?

As I mentioned in the Articles Section, every language has some aspects that seem to have little rhyme or reason and are therefore so difficult as to be nearly impossible for anyone but native speakers, thus allowing people to distinguish the in-group from the out-group. This section will deal with such a feature – the choice between gerund and infinitive after certain verbs.

http://grammar.ccc.commnet.edu/grammar/verblist.htm

The web link above contains color-coded tables of verbs that take infinitives (green), object + infinitive (pink), gerunds (blue), or preposition + gerund (purple). These lists are not all-inclusive, but they represent the most common verbs that are particular with respect to gerunds or infinitives. Some verbs, like *remember*, can take either a gerund or an infinitive, but the choice will lead to different meanings.

Consider the following sentences.

11. The doctor could not remember locking the door.
12. The doctor could not remember to lock the door.

What's the difference between these two sentences? (Hint: every day versus on a particular day).

How about these two?

13. The student stopped to buy coffee.
14. The student stopped buying coffee.

These two have nearly opposite meanings, don't they?

The trouble with choosing between a gerund or an infinitive is that there is no rule for discerning[53] which to choose. The *verb + gerund or verb + infinitive* collocations must be memorized or learned from use.

Learning from reading, listening to, and communicating in English is the more enjoyable way, so when you are reading, highlight the verb + gerund/infinitive collocations you come across in a span of 5 or 6 pages. It can be a very instructive exercise.

> ✓ **Writing tip:** Notice and highlight verb + gerund/infinitive collocations when you read.

Look at the website above and see which ones you already know, and which ones you do not. Make a list of those you do not already know, and try to memorize them.

---

53 discerning: figuring out

Exercise 2

Complete the following sentences using a gerund or an infinitive and whatever is necessary to complete the thought.

  a. Students should avoid _____ .
  b. It is important not to hesitate[54] _____ .
  c. The law will prohibit _____ .
  d. Teachers must not excuse _____ .
  e. A child should not be permitted _____ .
  f. It is difficult to imagine _____ .
  g. International students often complain_____ .
  h. The contract appears _____ .
  i. The senator did not recall _____ .
  j. The astronauts are preparing _____ .

Exercise 3

Try the following. Be sure to use gerunds or infinitives in each blank with whatever else is necessary.

  a. By _____, I will be able _____ without _____ .
  b. Instead of _____, students should _____ .
  c. In order _____, it is necessary _____ .
  d. _____ will prevent _____ .

D. PARALLEL STRUCTURE WITH GERUNDS AND INFINITIVES

In a sentence with a list, all elements must be parallel (the same part of speech). Errors in parallelism with gerunds and infinitives are relatively common. Consider the following sentence.

  15. Manjiro Nakahama enjoyed fishing, sailing, and to study engineering. X

Do you see the error here? How would you fix it?

---

54 hesitate: pause or delay

Exercise 4

Make sentences listing a triad of gerunds or infinitives to complete the sentences below.

    a. I remember _____
_____.

    b. The school does not allow students _____
_____.

    c. Doctors do not advise _____
_____.

Exercise 5

It's time to write. Write a paragraph about one of your parents, describing what they enjoy, avoid, encourage, and what you remember them doing or saying.

Unit 9 Subjunctives

Verbs like *recommend* and *suggest* can take gerunds. Consider the following sentences.

1. The travel agent recommended visiting the Northeast in the fall.
2. She also suggested bringing an umbrella in case of rain.

These sentences are perfect as they are. However, something strange happens when an agent is introduced, as in the sentences below.

3. The travel agent recommended her client visiting the Northeast in the fall. X
4. She also suggested the customer bringing an umbrella in case of rain. X

Sentences 3 and 4 are not correct. These sentences require the **subjunctive** as demonstrated below.

5. The travel agent recommended that her client visit the Northeast in the fall.
6. She also suggested that the customer bring an umbrella in case of rain.

Notice here that infinitives following *client* or *customer* in these sentences are also incorrect.

The subjunctive mood seems to be evolving out of American English, but there are two important instances when it used.

1. With *recommend, suggest, demand,* and *insist* (RSDI). We have already seen how this works with the first two. The last two are shown below.

   a. The surgeon insisted that the operation be performed immediately.
   b. The teacher demanded that the student complete the assignment by the next day.

The pattern is S + RSDI + that +agent noun + plain verb (no tense, helpers, or modals). The word *that* technically can be omitted, but I do NOT recommend omission because it leads to errors both in writing and in reading; that is, reducing *that* reduces clarity.

Other verbs such as *request, require, ask,* and *urge* can follow this pattern, but they do not have to. They can be completed with infinitival expressions. RSDI require the subjunctive if they are followed by an agent noun, but they can be written without the agent as in Sentences 1 and 2 above.

2. With It is *important/essential/crucial/critical/necessary/vital* that …
Notice that these adjectives all basically mean "important." The pattern is as follows:

It is important* that + agent noun + plain verb (no tense, helpers, or modals).

   a. It is essential that students submit their writing to turnitin.com.
   b. It is vital to national security that the new class of submarine be developed.

The subjunctive mood is relatively rare, but it is vital that it be used with recommendations and statements of importance. Again, *that* may be reduced, but it leads to confusion.

Exercise 1

Write a short paragraph including a triad of suggestions/recommendations for improving Main Street.

Exercise 2

Write another short paragraph stressing the importance of reducing, reusing, and recycling in preserving the environment.

Unit 10 Adjectives and Adjective Clauses

A. ADJECTIVES

Adjectives describe nouns. They typically either come before nouns or after a linking verb, as in the sentence below.

     1. Scary movies may be harmful to the psychological development of children.

Scary and *psychological* come before the nouns *movies* and *development*, respectively, and *harmful* follows the linking verb *be*.

Generally speaking, using adjectives is not so difficult for the advanced student, but there are a couple of tricky areas. First, several adjectives seem to be erroneously[55] thought to be verbs, as in the following sentences.

     2. The students did not aware that there would be a test on the new material. X

     3. Chinese proud their rapid economic development. X

Aware and *proud* are adjectives, not verbs. How can Sentences 2 and 3 above be fixed? (Hint: *be* verbs, *of*)

Other adjectives, such as *trustable**, just do not exist. The proper word is *trustworthy.* Another issue with adjectives is that some adjectives take different forms, and it is difficult to determine which form to use. **Table 5** shows some common adjectives that have different forms.

Table 5: Adjectives with various forms

Causes to Feel	Feels
aggravating	aggravated
annoying	annoyed
boring	bored
dangerous	endangered
frightening	frightened
frustrating	frustrated
interesting	interested
relaxing	relaxed
scary	scared
stressful	stressed
surprising	surprised
thrilling	thrilled

Table 5 is not exhaustive, but it is sufficient to illustrate the point and to provide practice. Notice the headings of the two columns. An ***interesting* thing** causes the feeler to **feel *interested***, and so on for the

---

55 erroneously: mistakenly

rest of the table. Many students have been taught that a thing must be the noun described by the adjectives in Column 1, while a person must be described by the adjectives in Column 2. While this idea is somewhat helpful and works most of the time, it is not accurate, as illustrated in the following sentence.

4. The teacher is interesting because he is interested in the interests of his students and presents his material in ways that keep his students interested.

Here, the *teacher* (a person) is both *interesting* (he causes students to feel interested) and *interested* (he feels interest), while the students are *interested* (they feel interest.).

Exercise 1

Which of the following sentences are correct? How would you fix the incorrect ones?

a. This course is stressed for students because there is so much writing.

b. The bungee jumping is thrilling but somewhat endangered.

c. Students awared the robbery that occurred last week on campus.

d. Relaxed music may promote effective studying.

e. It may be surprising to many that clowns are often considered frightening.

f. The school is proud of its mascot56, even though many consider it annoyed.

Another problematic issue involving adjectives is erroneous usage such as in the following sentence.

5. Students are easy to commute by Uber. X

6. Parents are difficult to raise their children whey both parents work. X

These sentences can be corrected by using the academic sentence structure

It is <u>adjective</u> for <u>noun</u> to <u>verb.</u>

This structure can be used in place of the subjunctive structures in the Subjunctive section.

7. It is essential for students to use subjunctives properly.

Exercise 2

Correct Sentences 5 and 6 above in a. and b. below.

a.

b.

---

56 mascot: animal or symbol that represents a group

B. ADJECTIVE CLAUSES

Adjective clauses are clauses (they contain a subject and a verb) that act as adjectives; that is, they modify nouns. Consider the following sentence.

> 8. The university *that* was *ranked* the *highest* for programs *that were innovative and practical* received the lowest ratings for athletics.

The two adjective clauses are italicized. The first modifies *university*, and the second modifies *programs*.

What is the main subject of the entire sentence? What is the primary verb? Notice how the word that acts as the subject in each of the adjective clauses.

Adjective clauses are not always headed by *that*, as illustrated in the following sentences.

> 9. The professor *who* taught the class last year retired.
>
> 10. The place where the tournament was held was difficult to find.
>
> 11. Revolutions often occur at times when poverty is widespread.
>
> 12. *The Cop and the Anthem* is a short story in which the main character tries to go to jail but fails many times.
>
> 13. The computer on *which* I had written that paper crashed, so I lost it and all my other work.
>
> 14. Apples, *which* are the most popular fruit worldwide, are related to roses.

C. ESSENTIAL AND NON-ESSENTIAL CLAUSES

The adjective clauses in Sentences 9-13 are called **essential clauses** because they are essential to understanding which professor, place, times, story, or computer is being discussed. Prove this to yourself by covering up the adjective clauses and asking yourself, "Do I know which professor retired?" and so on.

The adjective clause in Sentence 14 is not essential to understanding which apples are being referred to, so it is set off by commas. The sentence is not talking about any particular apples at all. Rather, it is talking about apples in general. Now consider the following sentences.

> 15. His son, who is 26, is an accomplished guitarist.
>
> 16. His son who is 26 is an accomplished guitarist.

What can be inferred about the number of sons the man has in each of these sentences? In which sentence is there only one son? Which sentence implies that there are others? How do we know?

When the noun being referred to is already clearly identifiable either by name or context, and when the adjective clause is providing extra (non-essential) information, the clause is set off by commas. If the adjective clause is necessary to identify which item/person/idea is being discussed, no commas are used.

Going back to Sentence 12 and 13, did you notice the prepositions before *which*? Why were they there? (Hint: think of the fundamental sentences that were combined to create 12 and 12. Did they contain the same prepositions?)

D. *THAT* VS. *WHY, WHERE,* AND *IN WHICH*

Sometimes choices among headwords for adjective clauses are confusing. Consider the following sentences.

> 17. The reason that was provided was not satisfactory. (*why* will not work)
>
> 18. The reason why he limps is that he had polio as a child. (*that* will not work)
>
> 19. The classroom that is used is too cold. (*where* will not work)
>
> 20. The classroom where they study is too cold. (*that* will not work)
>
> 21. The play in which a jury deliberates is *Twelve Angry Men*. (*that* will not work)
>
> 22. The play that was performed last night was *Twelve Angry Men*.
>   (*in which* will not work.)

Can you infer the difference between *that* and the other three? *That* is used to describe the thing as a whole, whereas the other three introduce an explanation (in the case of *why*) or action that happens *within the thing.*

Exercise 3

Choose the proper word in the following sentences.

> a. The email (that/in which) arrived last night was from the CEO.
> b. The file (that/in which) contains the presentation is corrupt.
> c. The plane (that/in which) she flew was crowded. (two meanings)
> d. The park (that/where) she played as a child was made into a national monument.
> e. The restaurant (that/where) she enjoys most is The Blue Heron.
> f. The assignment (that/in which) was due yesterday was easy.
> g. The team lost the game (that/in which) she scored 30 points.

E. REDUCING ADJECTIVE CLAUSES

Some clauses can be reduced, while others may not. Take, for instance, Sentence c from Exercise 3. If the sentence means that she was the pilot, it can be reduced as follows.

> 23. The plane she flew was crowded. (*that* has been reduced)

However, if she was riding in the plane, the sentence below cannot be reduced.

> 24. The plane in which she flew was crowded.

Why? Reducing the second would result in Sentence 23, which has a different meaning.

Exercise 4

Sentences e and f in Exercise 3 can also be reduced. Reduce them in a and b, respectively, below.

    a. (e)

    b. (f)

Clauses that contain helping *be*-verbs can generally be reduced by removing *that* and the *be*-verb, as in the following sentences.

    25. The longest book (that was) written by Tolstoy was *War and Peace*.

    26. The man (who is) pacing on the sideline is the coach.

Notice that Sentences a and b in Exercise 3 cannot be reduced because *that* is the subject of the clause, and there is no *be*-verb to remove with it. **Basically, for every subject in a sentence, there must be a verb, and vice-versa, so if removing a that leaves a verb with no subject, it cannot be reduced.** (Notice that *–ing* forms without *be* and past participles are not considered verbs; they function more like adjectives).

Why is reducing important? It is useful in paraphrasing or economizing. If an original text is reduced, a paraphrase may expand the clause. The reverse is also true; if an original text has expanded clauses, they may be reduced in a paraphrase. To economize words, as in an abstract that must meet a word limit, authors will usually reduce clauses as much as possible to pack more information into the abstract in fewer words.

However, reducing is sometimes dangerous, as it can lead to ambiguity. Consider the following sentence.

    27. The boy passed many office workers running to catch the train.

Who was running to catch the train? Do you see the ambiguity? It can be either the boy or the office workers.

Exercise 5

To eliminate the ambiguity, what are the two ways in which Sentence 27 can be expanded? The meanings are provided.

    a. (the boy is running) _____ _____.

    b. (the office workers are running) _____.

F. SUCH AS

The phrase *such as* is a little difficult to classify. It basically means *that includes* or *including*, which are adjective clauses, or *like*, which is a preposition. In any case, it is adjectival in nature, and advanced students do tend to struggle somewhat with it, so it is included here. The following sentences show some of the common errors involving *such as*.

28. Refugees arrive from numerous regions that are experiencing political, economic, or social problems such as Africa, the Middle East, or Central Asia. X

29. Such as Africa, the Middle East, or Central Asia. X

The construction of Sentence 28 makes it seem like Africa and the other regions are examples of *problems* because that is the noun that most immediately precedes them. How can this sentence be corrected? The *such as* phrase ideally should immediately follow the word it is describing. In this case, it should come after *regions*, as shown in Sentence 30 below.

30. Refugees arrive from numerous regions such as Africa, the Middle East, or Central Asia, wherever political, social, or economic problems cause them to flee.

Sentence 29 really is not a sentence at all, as it is a fragment. Also, a sentence will never begin with *Such as*.

Exercise 6

Create sentences using *such as* that describe the following topics. The first has been done for you.

a. chronic illnesses related to obesity
   Chronic illnesses such as atherosclerosis[57], hypertension[58], and diabetes are all related to obesity.
b. b. foods that can be found in most student dorm rooms
c. c. holidays on which families tend to gather
d. d. sports that are popular in your country but not in the U. S.

G. DEFINITIONS

Adjective clauses commonly used in definitions. Consider the following definition of a pickle.

> A pickle is a cucumber or other vegetable that has been soaked in a solution that is so high in salinity[59], acidity, or both that bacteria cannot grow. Pickles have shelf-lives that far exceed those of fresh vegetables, so pickling is a practical way to provide food in the winter. Pickles also pack flavor that far exceeds their volume because of the salt

---

57 atherosclerosis: narrowed arteries
58 hypertension: high blood pressure
59 salinity: saltiness

or acid in which they have been soaked. Therefore, they are often used on sandwiches or in salads sold in delis.

Exercise 7

Highlight the adjective clauses in the above definition.

    a. How many adjective clauses did you find?
    b. How many were reduced? Which one(s)?
    c. Could any others have been reduced? Which one(s)?

Exercise 8

Choose two of the following and write a paragraph definition similar in length to the one above.

    a. a supervisor
    b. a hamburger
    c. a vacation
    d. an emergency room
    e. a passport
    f. the greenhouse effect

Exercise 9

Personal statements: Complete the following in a way the might impress a college entrance official. The completions will begin with a relative clause.

    a. I will never forget the day
    a. I once met an inspiring person

H. MODIFYING CLAUSAL MEANING RATHER THAN A WORD

Sometimes adjective clauses may refer to the meaning of a preceding clause or sentence as a whole, instead of modifying a particular word. Consider the following sentence about pickles.

    29. Pickles are soaked in solutions with high acidity or salinity, which enables them to last a long time.

What does *which* refer to? It is the entire idea of pickles being treated with salt or acid, and not any particular word. Care must be taken when writing in this manner. Sometimes the meaning becomes unclear. Academic writing does contain these sorts or adjective clauses, and they should always start with a comma. However, clearer writing may be as follows:

30. Pickles are soaked in solutions with high acidity or salinity. This process, referred to as pickling, enables them to last a long time.

Exercise 10

Compare Sentences 29 and 30 to answer the following questions.

    a. Which do you think is clearer, Sentence 29 or 30?
    b. Which is more efficient?
    c. Which is generally more important, clarity or efficiency?
    d. In what circumstances might each be chosen?

Exercise 11

Complete the following sentences with adjective clauses that refer to the prior clause as a whole.

    a. Trump won the presidential election of 2016,
    a. Global temperatures continue to rise,
    a. Stock market prices have risen consistently since 2016,
    a. A new antibiotic[60]-resistant bacteria has been discovered,

Exercise 12

Orally paraphrase your sentences in Exercise 11 to make them clearer.

---

60 antibiotic: a drug that kills bacteria

Unit 11 Coordinating Conjunctions and Transitions

Usage of coordinating conjunctions and transitions is usually fairly well developed by the time students reach the advanced level, but there is an assortment of errors that typically continue to appear in writing at high levels. This unit will address those issues.

A. STARTING SENTENCES WITH FANBOYS

Beginning sentences with *for, and, nor, but, or, yet,* and *so* (FANBOYS) is somewhat frowned upon in academic writing because it gives the writing an informal run-on or fragmented feel. Many textbooks, including this one, will occasionally start sentences with one of the FANBOYS, but they do so to gain attention, to deliberately be informal, or for other such pedagogical (teaching) purposes. And when they do (I am doing it now), there is no comma after the FANBOYS conjunction.

> ✓ **Writing tip:** Unless you are already an accomplished writer, it is advisable not to start a sentence with *for, and, nor, but,* or, *yet,* or *so.* Instead, use a more academic conjunction, or connect the first clause to a previous sentence.

B. COMMA SPLICE RUN-ON SENTENCES

Consider the following sentences. One of them has an error in it. Which one is it, and why? Write an X after the incorrect one.

1. Ducks swim and fly.

2. Ducks swim quickly, and they can also fly long distances.

3. Ducks swim, they also fly.

Sentence 3 is incorrect because it has connected two independent clauses with only a comma. This type of error is called a **comma splice**, and university writing instructors tend to have an exaggerated[61] distaste for them because native language writers make the same sort of error. (Native writers do not tend to struggle with tenses and articles so much, so comma splice errors may seem more annoying than they should.) How can Sentence 3 be fixed? (Hint: use a different punctuation mark)

Consider three grammatically correct ways to express the same idea.

4. Ducks swim; they also fly.

5. Ducks swim, and they also fly.

6. Ducks swim. They also fly.

---

61 exaggerated: over-emphasized

Which of the three seems more sophisticated? Why? Sentence 4 is more sophisticated because using a semicolon properly is a relatively advanced skill, but each type has its own purpose. Sentence 4 is sophisticated, 5 seems ordinary, and 6 may be used to draw attention to the fact that ducks fly by deliberate use of the simple, short sentence.

✓ **Writing tip:** Skillful academic writers use a variety of sentence types. Using a semi-colon to combine independent clauses displays sophistication. Using an occasional short, simple sentence adds emphasis and draws attention to the point being made.

C. FRAGMENTS

Fragments are incomplete sentences. Sentences beginning with one of the FANBOYS conjunctions are usually considered fragments. Another major type of fragment is the *for example* fragment, as illustrated below.

7. For example, freedom of the press, freedom of speech, and freedom of assembly[62]. X

Notice that even though this *sentence* is long, it has no verb; thus, it is a fragment, not a sentence. A simple fix for this fragment is shown in Sentence 8.

8. Some examples are freedom of the press, freedom of speech, and freedom of assembly.

D. MORE ACADEMIC CONJUNCTIONS

For = Because, Since
And = Also, Moreover, In addition, Furthermore,
But = However,
Or = Otherwise,
Yet = However,
So = Therefore, Thus, Hence, Consequently,

Academic conjunctions are typically used at the beginning of a sentence or a clause, and they are followed by a comma. When used at the head of a clause that is not the beginning of a sentence, a semicolon usually precedes them, as illustrated in the sentences below.

9. Electric cars emit no harmful gases; moreover, they are quiet.

10. Nebraska played more aggressively than Penn State did; thus, they won the game.

11. A parking sticker is necessary for that lot; otherwise, cars may be towed.

12. Freedom of speech is a precious right; however, it is often misused.

Notice how the semi-colon is used before the conjunction and a comma is placed after it.

---

62 freedom of assembly: freedom to gather

E. CONFUSION AMONG ACADEMIC CONJUNCTIONS

Below are groups of conjunctions, but one word in each group is unlike the others. Identify the different one and explain why.

> a. also, besides, in addition, moreover
> b. although, even though, notwithstanding
> c. in contrast, on the other hand, on the contrary

In item a, *besides* is different. *Besides* tends to be used to indicate an afterthought or a less significant idea, similar to "Oh, and by the way" in speech. It is generally overused by ESL writers.

In item b, *notwithstanding* is different because it is used with a noun (phrase), but not a clause, as illustrated below.

> 13. The winter snow notwithstanding, the climate of Philadelphia is pleasant.

> 14. Even though it snows in the winter, the climate of Philadelphia is pleasant.

In item c, *on the contrary* is different in that it implies negation, not just difference. It is used to shift from what is *not* true to what *is* true.

> 15. Immigrants do not typically ruin a country; on the contrary, they typically strengthen it.

Notice that *in fact* could actually be used in Sentence 15 as well.

F. IDIOMATIC MISTAKES

What is idiomatically incorrect in the following sentences?

> 16. Freedom is a self-contradictory concept: in the one hand, it allows individuals to do what they want; in the other hand, they may not do what they want because they must control themselves. X

> 17. On the one side, cities are convenient; on the other side, they may be dangerous. X

The correct idioms are **on the one hand** and **on the other hand**.

A. WHEREAS

Whereas is a wonderful word used to introduce a contrast. Advanced ESL students tend to not use it enough. It is used as follows.

> 18. Whereas the focus in Japanese sentences tends to be at the end, the focus in English sentences tends to be at the beginning.
> 19. This grammar book is short, whereas most of the others I have seen are long.

The comma in Sentence 19 seems to inspire some debate. Overall, it might be safer to use it than to not use it. (Notice the hedging.)

B. USING SIMPLISTIC TRANSITIONS

Typically, non-native writers of English tend to use more transition words than native writers do, and they also tend to use them in simpler ways. Here, attention will be drawn to the use of *first, second, third* and *first, next, last* progressions. Consider the following paragraph.

Paragraph 1

The moon affects the earth in three major ways. First, it influences how fast the earth turns, slowing it down dramatically. Second, it creates the tides[63] by its gravitational pull. Third, it seems to influence the psychology of humans and the activity of other species.

Paragraph 2

The moon affects the earth in three major ways. Perhaps the most important effect is that the moon slows down the rotation speed of the earth dramatically. An additional major effect is that the moon creates the tides by its gravitational pull. The third and often overlooked effect of the moon on the earth is that it influences human psychology as well as the behavior of other species.

Compare the two paragraphs. Which seems more academic? Why? How and where are those transition words used? Notice how the transition words or forms of the words are incorporated within clauses in Paragraph 2, as opposed to being placed at the beginning of the sentences in Paragraph 1.

✓ **Writing tip:** Incorporate transition words into clauses, not only at the head of the clause, to achieve greater sophistication.

Exercise 1

Choose one or more of the following topics and write a paragraph that contains a triad of ideas. Pay attention to your use of conjunctions and transition words.

a. For a university student, what are the advantages and disadvantages of living in a dormitory?

b. What are the advantages and disadvantages of driving relative to walking?

c. What are the advantages and disadvantages of fast food?

---

63 tides: the rise and fall of oceans on the shore

Unit 12 Comparisons

A. GENERAL COMPARISONS

The language of comparisons can be quite complicated, but because comparing plays a crucial role in critical thinking, it is essential that college students be skilled in the necessary language. This unit will begin with some common errors.

> 1. Global warming is the same with the greenhouse effect. X
>
> 2. Global warming is same as the greenhouse effect. X
>
> 3. Football is similar with rugby. X

What's wrong with the sentences above? How can you fix them?

The idiomatic collocations are **be the same as,** and **be similar to.** <u>Repeat these out loud 5 times.</u>

Here is one more common error, but it is more complicated.

> 4. New Zealand has sheep more than people. X

Can you fix this one? (Hint: two words are inverted.) Sentence 5 is correct.

> 5. New Zealand has more sheep than people.

Notice that the object noun follows the comparative word (*more, less, fewer*).

Try one more. What's wrong with the following sentence?

> 6. The French class has less students than the Spanish class. X

Because *student* is a countable noun, *fewer* would be correct, even though many native speakers also make the same mistake.

With these word-level errors straightened out, we will move on to more complex issues. To make comparisons, data is often necessary, so it is provided in **Table 6.**

Table 6: Numbers of international students in Imaginary University (IU) (males/females T = total)

Year	Korean	Chinese	Saudi	Colombian
2000	50/50, T = 100	2/0, T = 2	1/0, T = 1	15/20, T = 35
2008	30/30, T = 60	40/10, T = 50	20/5, T = 25	10/15, T = 25
2016	5/5, T = 10	150/100, T = 250	80/40, T = 120	5/5, T = 10

Here are some comparisons that can be drawn from this data. Notice that specific numbers from the graph are not used; ratios such as *five times*, *one-fifth*, and *five-fold* are used instead.

7. In 2000, there were equal numbers of Korean men and Korean women.

8. The total number of Korean students at IU in 2016 was one-tenth that of 2000.

9. Coincidentally, the ratio of Korean men to Korean women was always the same.

10. In 2008, there were four times as many Chinese males as females at IU.

11. While the Korean population at IU in 2000 was nearly three times the Colombian, the two populations experienced similar downward trends.

12. In 2016, there were 50% more Chinese men at IU than Chinese women.

13. The number of Saudi students at IU increased nearly five-fold from 2008 to 2016.

Exercise 1

Use Table 6 to create sentences comparing the populations provided.

a. Chinese men and women in 2008.

b. Chinese students in 2016 versus 2008.

c. Colombian students in 2016 versus 2000.

d. Korean students versus Chinese students in 2000.

e. Colombian men and women in 2016

f. Saudi women in 2016 versus 2008

g. Korean men in 2016 versus 2008.

Exercise 2

Choose the correct words in the following paragraph.

One major trend was that there [1](are/were) far [2](fewer/less) Korean students in [3](2000/2016) than in [4](2000/2016) at IU. The trend was [5](same/similar) for Colombians. The Korean population decreased by 90 [6](percent/percentage), while the Colombian population decreased by [7](more than/nearly) 60 percent.

Exercise 3

Now write a paragraph of your own based on Table 6, starting with the phrase provided and referring to Chinese and Saudi populations.

On the other hand,

B. COMPARISONS WITH OUT- VERBS

One class of verbs is especially useful in making comparisons: *out-* verbs. These verbs consist of the prefix *out* added to another verb. They mean **to _____ more (better) than**. **Table 7** presents some common *out-* verbs.

Table 7: Useful academic out- verbs

outnumber	outclass	outrun	outrank	outproduce
outweigh	outlive	outplay	outlast	outsmart*
outperform	outsell	outscore	outvote	outwit*

* *smart* is an adjective, but *outsmart* is a verb, so it is included in this table.

* *wit* is a noun, but *outwit* is a verb.

Exercise 4

Consider the meanings of the following sentences. What does the *out-* verb mean in each one?

    a. Domestic students outperformed international students by only a slight margin.

    b. Democrats outvoted Republicans in the latest local election.

    c. Rommel was notorious[64] for his ability to outsmart his opponents.

Exercise 5

Choose the appropriate verb from Table 7 to complete the sentences below. Be sure to use the proper tense.

    a. The goal of any manufacturing company is to _____ and _____its competitors.

    b. Surprisingly, the BMW did not _____ the Honda in road tests.

    c. Battery A _____ Battery B by 25% in the experiment.

    d. Longevity data reveals that in general, women _____ men by 5 years.

    e. The advantages _____ the disadvantages.

    f. Usain Bolt easily _____ the competition in the 100-meter dash.

    g. That luxury hotel simply _____ this roadside motel in every way.

    h. The champions _____ their opponent convincingly and _____ them 6 to 1.

---

64 notorious: famous in a negative way

Exercise 6

Using data from Table 6 or from your own imagination, create two more comparisons using *out-*verbs. The first is done for you.

    a. In 2000, Korean students outnumbered Chinese students by a ratio of 50:1.

    b. _____

        _____

        _____

    c. _____

        _____

        _____

Unit 13 Adverbs and Adverbial Clauses

Adverbs or **adverbial clauses** describe how, why, where, when, or to what degree something is done. Adverb placement was dealt with in passing in the Modals unit, but in general, adverb placement is somewhat flexible, so placement is not one of the major issues advanced students experience with adverbs. This unit will deal with using adverbs to increase efficiency of writing, to hedge, and to boost meaning. It will also address the tricky issue of beginning sentences with negative adverbs. Then it will address adverbial clauses.

A. INCREASING EFFICIENCY WITH ADVERBS

Consider the following sentence.

> 1. Adolescents experience changes in psychological, physical, and social aspects. X

This sentence is somewhat awkward in the use of *aspects*. It can be much improved by employing adverbs as shown in Sentence 2.

> 2. Adolescents change psychologically, physically, and socially.

Sentence 2 is considerably more concise and does not seem awkward.

Exercise 1

Improve the following sentences.

   a. In the stomach, food is digested in ways that are physical and chemical in nature.
   b. Politicians should be certain that what they say is correct both with respect to politics and with respect to facts.
   c. Children of illegal refugees tend to struggle with education, in economics, and in social relationships.

B. HEDGING WITH ADVERBS

Hedging was addressed in the Modals section, but adverbs are also important in hedging.

Consider the following sentences.

> 3. Michael Jordan is arguably the greatest basketball player who ever lived, even though he was cut as a sophomore from his high school basketball team.

> 4. Michael Jordan is likely the greatest basketball player ever.

Notice the adverbs *arguably* and *likely*. These words soften the statements, protecting them from critical attack. An argument certainly can be made whether the Michael Jordan is "the greatest."

Academic adverbs that are frequently used to hedge statements include *arguably, likely, probably, possibly, perhaps, somewhat, virtually* (before *all/every*), *practically* (before *all/every*), and others.

Exercise 2

Create a sentence with a hedging adverb for the following topics. Use a different word each time.

   a. sugar, dangerous food ingredient
   b. all medicines can produce side-effects
   c. every lawyer faces ethical65 dilemmas
   d. Jimmy Carter, the most misunderstood American president

C. BOOSTING WITH ADVERBS

Adverbs can also be used to emphasize or strengthen what is being said, driving home a point. Consider the following sentence.

   5. Clearly, the coach was out of line when he struck the referee.

The adverb *clearly* boosts the meaning of the sentence. Academic boosting adverbs include *even, actually, certainly, definitely, obviously, emphatically, assuredly*, and others.

Exercise 3

Create a sentence with a boosting adverb for the following topics. Use a different word each time.

   a. water, essential for life
   b. education deserves a greater portion of the budget
   c. being absent → failure
   d. Dogs, smarter than cats
   e. English skill → higher salaries

D. FRONTING NEGATIVE ADVERBS

As stated a couple times earlier, focus in English is usually at the beginning of the sentence, and to emphasize a certain word or phrase, authors will often choose to **front** it, or move it to the beginning of the sentence. However, something peculiar happens to the sentence when negative adverbs are fronted. Consider the following sentences.

---

65 ethical: related to right and wrong

6. Arizona seldom receives rain.

7. Seldom does Arizona receive rain.

Both of these sentences say are grammatically correct, and they communicate the same idea, but the focus is different. What is the difference? (Hint: look at the first word)

However, the grammar is different as well. Why does Sentence 7 have *does*? The answer is that when adverbs that are negative in meaning are fronted, the subject and verb of the main clause are inverted. **In other words, after a fronted negative adverb, the sentence will look like a question, even though it is not a question.** Negative adverbs that are commonly fronted in academic writing include *not only, only, only _____, seldom, rarely, not until,* and *rarely. Only _____* is illustrated below.

8. Only in leap years are presidential elections held in the United States.

9. Only if patients or their guardians sign consent forms can surgery be performed.

With *not only ... (but) also*, perhaps the most commonly used negative adverb expression, care must be taken where the *also* is placed.

10. Not only can Manning play football, he can also host a comedy show skillfully.

Notice that *but* has been reduced and that *also* is after the modal.

Exercise 4

Create sentences starting with the following negative adverbs about the topics in parentheses.

    a. Not only … also (animals communicate, use tools)
    b. Rarely (weather)
    c. Only once (someone apologized)
    d. Seldom (homework)
    e. Not until the 1990s (computers)

E. ADVERBIAL CLAUSES

Adverbial clauses contain a subject and a verb, and they play the roles of regular adverbs, telling how, why, where, when, or to what degree something happens or is done. Similar to adjective clauses, they can often be reduced, making the subject and verb of the clause not apparent. This reducibility is helpful when paraphrasing or when attempting to write more concisely.

While using adverbial clauses may not be particularly difficult, there are some pitfalls to avoid.

I. Fragments

Adverb clauses are dependent clauses, so they cannot be used separate from an independent clause. A common error among advanced students is to create a fragment by using adverbial clauses by themselves, as illustrated in the erroneous *sentences* below.

> 11. When the poet was composing her poem. X
>
> 12. If the amendment[66] to the law had not been added. X
>
> 13. Even though the hurricane was not as powerful as predicted. X

Sentences 11-13 are all fragments.

II. *While/During*

Clauses/phrases with *while* and *during* can be tricky to use correctly. A *while* clause can be completed by a subject and verb or by a reduction resulting in an *–ing* phrase, as illustrated below.

> 14. While students are studying for exams, chewing gum may help them memorize more effectively.
>
> 15. While studying for exams, students may find that chewing gum helps them memorize more effectively. (reduced)

Notice that the reduced sentence (15) is not actually shorter because the subject had to be explicitly stated in the main clause and the rest of the clause had to be rearranged somewhat. Also notice that the subject in the main clause (*students*) had to match the implied subject of *studying* in the reduced clause. When those two subjects do not match, it results in a **dangling participle**, which will be addressed a little later.

During cannot be completed with a clause at all, whether reduced or not. *During* is followed by a noun (phrase) as shown below.

> 16. During the exam, the fire alarm rang, resulting in chaos and an ultimate rescheduling of the test.

III. *Although … , Even though …*

The clause after an *although* or *even though clause* will **not** begin with *but*. The meaning of *but* is included within *although* and *even though*, so using *but* would be redundant[67]. Proper use is illustrated in Sentence 17.

> 17. Although the President Kennedy was rushed to surgery, he died shortly thereafter.

---

66 amendment: a change to a law that occurs after it was passed
67 redundant: repetitive

IV. *In spite of/Despite/Because of/Due to*

In spite of, *despite*, *because of*, and *due to* serve as prepositions; that means that similar to *during*, they are followed by noun (phrases) and **not** clauses. They cannot be followed by a subject with a verb to make a clause.

V. Dangling participles

Consider the following erroneous sentence.

> 18. While investigating the crime scene for footprints, it started raining. X

This sentence makes it sound like the weather (*it*) was investigating the crime scene. Sentence 19 (below) illustrates how to correct this dangling participle (mismatch of subjects between the participle and main clause).

> 19. While detectives were investigating the crime scene for footprints, it starting raining.

The dangling participle in Sentence 18 resulted from reducing the adverbial clause. The lesson to be learned is that care is necessary when reducing adverbial clauses.

VI. Reducing adverbial clauses

The sentences below illustrate how to reduce adverbial clauses.

> 20. When champions face adversity, they dig deep into their hearts and find the power to reach an entirely different level. (expanded)
> 21. (When) facing adversity, champions dig deep into their hearts and find the power to reach an entirely different level. (reduced)
> 22. While the mountain climber was descending the mountain, he stumbled[68] and injured his knee. (expanded)
> 23. (While) descending the mountain, the mountain climber stumbled and injured his knee. (reduced).

Notice that the subject is removed, the verb becomes the *–ing* form, and the subject is explicitly stated in the main clause.

---

68 stumbled: tripped

Exercise 1

Which of the following sentences are correct, and which are not? Correct the incorrect ones.

a. Due to the snow accumulated 12 inches, classes were canceled.
b. Because the roads were covered with ice, transportation was extremely dangerous.
c. Despite cold weather, children enjoyed playing in the snow.
d. Although snow plows worked all night to remove the snow.
e. Even though salt was poured on the streets, but the ice did not melt due to the extreme cold.
f. During the snow fell, power outages also occurred in the city.
g. While the electricity was out, some looting occurred as well.
h. In order to control the looting, the governor of the state called for the National Guard.
i. Wherever the soldiers went, order was quickly restored.
j. Watching the falling snow, sirens were heard throughout the city.

Exercise 2

Complete the following sentences.

a. Everywhere the president visited _____
_____.

b. The bridge was built so (that) __ _____
_____.

c. Although writing assignments are difficult, _____
_____.

d. Because the president had promised to reduce taxes, _____
_____.

e. When _____, the instructor _____
_____.

f. Although many _____, few _____
_____.

g. Despite the fact that _____, _____
_____.

h. Up until now, _____, but from now on _____
_____.

Unit 14 Conditionals

Conditionals are usually thought of as *if*-statements, although *unless* is also a conditional indicator. Conditions are somewhat tricky in that they can be **real** (truly possible or practical) or **unreal** (purely hypothetical, or only in the imagination). Conditional sentences employ modals, so principles from that unit will be recycled here.

A. REAL CONDITIONALS

Consider the following sentences.

1. If a divorced man remarries, his life expectancy tends to increase.

2. However, if a divorced woman remarries, her life expectancy tends to decrease.

These sentences are dealing with present situations. The writer is communicating essential conclusions from a study. Thus, the present tense is used in all clauses.

Now, consider the following sentences.

3. Unless a seed is planted, it will not grow.

4. If fields are not enriched with fertilizer[69], crop yields will decrease.

These sentences describe real cause-effect relationships, with a present cause leading to a future effect. Notice how the present tense is used in the *if*–clause, and *will* was inserted into the independent clause. For hedging, *may* could also be used instead of *will* in Sentence 4.

B. UNREAL CONDITIONALS

Consider the following sentences.

5. If pets could talk, they would probably tell hilarious[70] tales about their owners.

6. If they told such stories, they would likely laugh so much they would not need exercise.

Here the conditional is purely hypothetical. Pets can't talk. (Oh, but if they could …) In this case, the *if*-clause contains the past form of the modal or main verb, and then the independent clause is marked by *would*. (*Could* or *might* can also be used to mark the verbs in the independent clause, but not in Sentences 5 or 6 because of the adverbs *probably* and *likely*.)

C. PAST CONDITIONALS

This conditional is the difficult one because the verb combinations can become long. Consider the following sentences.

---

69 fertilizer: a substance that makes soil richer
70 hilarious: extremely funny

7. If the winters of Russia had not been so severe, the armies of Napoleon or Hitler might have been victorious.

8. Also, if the invaders had been clever enough not to invade in the fall, the outcomes could have been different.

9. It would have been wiser still if Napoleon and Hitler had never invaded Russia at all.

These past conditionals employ the **past perfect** in the **if-clause** (one of the rare cases in which that tense is used), and *would, could* or *might* in the main clause plus the **present perfect**. It is easy to get confused using these perfect tenses.

Exercise 1

Notice the form of the *if*-clause and complete the following sentences appropriately.

   a. If humans did not have to eat,
   b. If fossil fuels run out,
   c. Unless children are educated,
   d. If cancer research receives greater funding,
   e. If Yao Ming had not played in the NBA,
   f. If bacteria did not exist,

So far only sentences have been constructed. To write a paragraph related to a conditional, every verb within that conditional situation must be marked appropriately for reality/unreality.

For instance, taking Sentence a in Exercise 1 as a starting point, the following paragraph might result.

If humans *did not have* to eat, much of human culture *would not* exist because so much of culture <u>is</u> related to food. Agriculture, food shopping, restaurants, ethnic cooking, and meals themselves *would not exist*. Holidays *would not involve* holiday foods and meals shared. Other holiday activities <u>would have developed</u> to replace eating, but it <u>is</u> difficult to imagine what those activities *might be*.

Notice how the italicized verbs follow the form of the unreal conditional, marked with *would*. However, the underlined verbs are different. Why? Think about it for a while.

The <u>is</u> in the second line expresses a truth that is always true; it is not subject to the condition, so it takes the present tense. For the second <u>is</u>, the writer removes himself from the conditional situation and writes about the fact that it is now hard for him to imagine. That shift requires the shift to the present tense. What happened with <u>would have developed</u>? Why does this shift to the past conditional? There is an implied conditional in that sentence: if food customs <u>had not been necessary</u>.

Exercise 2

Take two of the sentences in Exercise 1 and develop them into paragraphs.

D. *EVEN IF* AND *EVEN THOUGH*

Students often ask about the difference between *even if* and *even though*. Basically, *even if* is used when the author **does not know** the condition. *Even though* is used when the condition is known. The following sentences illustrate this difference.

10. Even though it rained several nights last week, monthly rainfall is below normal.

11. Even if it rains again tonight night, monthly rainfall will be below normal.

In Sentence 10, the author knew it had rained. In Sentence 11, the author does not know whether or not it will rain that night.

One might also think that *even though* is used with past events, whereas *even if* is used with future events, but that is not exactly the case. Consider this situation.

12. Chinese was not offered in that high school, but even if it had been offered, few students would have taken it.

This sentence imagines the possibility of Chinese having been offered in the past, even though it was not actually offered.

Exercise 3

Complete the following sentences.

Even if the course is difficult, _____

_____

Even though the doctor wrote a prescription, _____

_____

g. Even though the plane took off on time, _____

_____

h. Even if simultaneous[71] language translating devices are invented, _____

_____

i. Even if the Apollo spacecraft had not landed on the moon, _____

_____

_____

71 simultaneous: at the same time

Unit 15 Noun Clauses

Noun clauses are clauses (they contain a subject and a verb) that fulfill the roles in sentences that ordinary nouns do. They can be subjects, objects of verbs, objects of prepositions, and complements. They can be somewhat tricky because many noun clauses start with question words (*why, where, when, who,* how), but the subject and verbs are **not** inverted as with questions. Subjects come before verbs in noun clauses as they do in normal clauses.

The following sentences demonstrate a variety of uses of noun clauses.

1. What happened to Amelia Earhart, the American aviation[72] pioneer[73], is still a mystery. (subject of the sentence)

2. No one knows how or where she disappeared. (object of the verb)

3. In fact, there is still debate about whether she died in a crash or whether she went on to live in obscurity. (objects of the preposition about)

4. It seems that her mystery will never be solved. (complement)

Notice:

- how first words of the clauses arc question words, *that* or *whether* (*if* is also an option, but *whether* seems to be preferred in academic writing)

- that subjects come before verbs in the clauses

- that there is only one headword (question words, *that* or *whether*) per clause

Read the following paragraph and highlight all the noun clauses.

Paragraph 1

It is well known that the longest days of the summer occur around June 22 in the Northern Hemisphere, and that the shortest days of winter occur around December 21. It is also commonly recognized that the hottest days of summer north of the equator typically do not occur until late July or even August. Similarly, it is often observed that the coldest days of winter do not usually occur until February. However, why the lags[74] between extremes of day length and extremes of temperature exist is seldom contemplated[75]. When asked about this phenomenon, most college students reply that they do not know. The principle that explains the day length/temperature phenomenon is that the earth acts as a heat reservoir[76]. When the days are the longest, the earth absorbs heat, removing it from the atmosphere. The result is that

---

72 aviation: flying
73 pioneer: a person who does something before others do it
74 lags: differences in time
75 contemplated: thought about
76 reservoir: something that stores another thing

in June, the air temperature is relatively cool. Then in late July or August, as the days shorten, the earth releases its heat, causing the atmosphere to be warmed by both the sun and the earth, resulting in higher temperatures. In winter, when the days are the shortest, the earth continues releasing its heat until February, which is when the coldest temperatures occur.

Did you find nine, seven of which were *that*-clauses, with one *why*-clause and one *when*-clause? What roles in the sentences do they play?

Exercise 1

Complete the following sentences.

a. It is difficult to understand _____
_____.

b. Few would have predicted _____
_____.

c. Few parents realize _____
_____.

d. I often wonder _____
_____.

e. It is clear _____
_____.

f. It is unclear _____
_____.

g. _____is what researchers need to find out.

Exercise 2

Choose one of the two prompts below and write a short paragraph using at least two noun clauses.

a. Should fast food be banned?
b. Should space exploration be a high priority?

Unit 16 Reported Speech

Reported speech in academic writing is used primarily when citing sources, as the following sentences demonstrate.

1. Dungy and Whitaker (2011) present their perspective on coaching and discuss the idea that coaches should seek to develop the player, not just the skills.

2. According to Super Bowl winning coaches Dungy and Whitaker (2011), athletes should pursue deeper goals than winning.

3. Dungy and Whitaker claim that integrity and character are actually more important than victory (2011).

4. In 2011, Dungy and Whitaker wrote that day-to-day progress is not always discernible, but that it should always be a goal.

5. Some coaches believe that winning is everything, but many winning coaches disagree (Dungy & Whitaker, 2011).

6. Based on the opinions presented by Dungy and Whitaker (2011), it is reasonable to conclude that the winning-is-everything approach to sports is misguided at best, and possibly quite dangerous.

Notice the following:

- *Presents* and *discusses* are **not** followed by *that-* noun clauses; they are followed by nouns which may be modified by adjective clauses.

- *According to Dungy and Whitaker,* _____ means "Dungy and Whitaker say (or said) _____." It would be redundant (incorrect) to write, "According to Dungy and Whitaker (2011), *they said that …*"

- In APA format, if the name of the author is written in the text, only the year should appear within the citation parentheses.

- The present tense is often preferred for reported speech, unless when the claim was made is written explicitly in the text (as in Sentence 4), the author cited is known to have died, or the author cited is known to have changed opinions and the former opinion is being reported.

- Skill with noun clauses is vital for reported speech (Sentences 3, 4, 5, 6).

- *Based on* is different from *according to*. *Based on* is often followed by evidence and then a conclusion, whereas *according to* Z merely means that Z said something.

A. REPORTING VERB PECULIARITIES

Certain reporting verbs can be followed by *that-* noun clauses, while others cannot. Table 8 contains a partial list of reporting verbs.

Table 8: Common reporting verbs that do or do not take *that*- noun clauses.

Take *that*		Do NOT take *that*	
argues	recommends	considers	illustrates
asserts	remarks	contradicts	opposes
believes	reports	criticizes	praises
claims	speculates	debates	presents
concludes	states	describes	refutes
mentions	suggests	discusses	rejects
observes	urges	explores	supports

A useful on-line website for reporting verbs is

https://www.adelaide.edu.au/writingcentre/docs/learningGuide_verbsForReporting.pdf

B. DIRECT QUOTES

When writing academic compositions, it is a sophisticated touch to include pertinent, well-stated, quotes from experts. However, as a rule of thumb, direct quotes should not exceed 10% of the paper. The excessive presence of quotes suggests that the writer is unskilled in paraphrasing and original thought.

When directly quoting a source, there are three requirements in APA format.

1. The quote should be exactly what the source said.*
2. Quotation marks must be around the quotation.
3. A citation with page # or paragraph # (if there are no page numbers, as with some web documents) must be included.

*A quote may be altered to fit the grammar of the text into which it is inserted, but changes must be marked with brackets [ ]. Also, ellipses (…) may be used to leave out portions of a quote if no distortion of original meaning results.

Below are some examples

1. Dungy and Whitaker (2011) describes the "look squad" as a simulation that "helps the first team's players visualize how plays will work against the other team's" (p. 2).
2. "Perceptions don't win ball games" (Dungy & Whitaker, 2011, p. 12).
3. Dungy and Whitaker (2011) assert that "players [need] to look beyond perceptions and look at reality" (p. 12). (The original word was "needed," but it would have conflicted in tense with assert.)
4. Carnegie claimed that more friends can be made "in two weeks by genuinely showing interest in them than … in two years by trying to get them interested in you" (as cited in Dungy & Whitaker, 2011, p. 10).

Notice how the periods come after the citation, not after the quote.

Exercise 1

Which of the following sentences are incorrect, and why?

  a. According to Dungy and Whitaker, life is more important than football.
  b. Dungy and Whitaker (2011) present that coaching is about improving players, not merely improving skills.
  c. Dungy and Whitaker observe that some players are more concerned with perception than with reality (2011).
  d. Dungy and Whitaker (2011) discuss the necessity of a "look squad" on the practice field. (p. 2)
  e. Based on the observations of Dungy and Whitaker (2011), visualizing seems to be beneficial to athletes.
  f. Dungy and Whitaker consider reality more important than perception (2011).
  g. In 2011, Dungy and Whitaker write, "Perceptions don't win ball games" (p. 12).
  h. Dungy and Whitaker (2011) criticize that the approach to coaching that seeks winning above all else.

Exercise 2

Based on your understanding of the sentences in this unit that express some of the ideas of Coach Dungy and his assistant Whitaker, summarize his philosophy of coaching in a short paragraph, using reported speech and citation techniques.

Dungy, T., & Whitaker, N. (2011). *The one-year uncommon life daily challenge*. Carol Stream, IL: Tyndale Momentum.

Unit 17 Approaching an Academic Voice

While this section may not technically pertain to grammar, it does apply to word choice that can significantly alter the impression that a written piece creates. By choosing appropriate academic expressions for a relatively small number of words (~25), a writer can create a much more sophisticated voice and increase the impact of the composition. Try not to use the words to the left of the arrows below, but instead choose words to the right. The academic words will often have a much more specific or narrower meaning, which is one reason they are wiser choices. However, care must be taken to use the academic terms appropriately.

Simple Words →Academic Expressions

Adjectives:

good /better/best→ beneficial, helpful, high quality, appropriate, proper, healthy, nutritious, acceptable, satisfying, fulfilling

bad /worse/worst→ poor, harmful, unhealthy, detrimental, damaging, unacceptable, improper, dangerous, (lack of___)

big → large, enormous, significant, major, great, widespread,

small → minor, insignificant, unimportant, few (a small number)

many → numerous, various, a variety of, a great number of, a multitude of, a plethora of, a myriad of, innumerable, several

much →an abundance of, a great amount of, a high concentration of

a lot of (see *many* and *much*, depending on whether the noun is countable or not) → [common: pervasive, widespread, considerable, appreciable]

hard→ difficult, complicated, arduous

hardworking → diligent

Verbs:

go back → return

go up → rise, increase, skyrocket, jump

go down →decrease, diminish, decline, drop, fall, plummet [fall dramatically]

get → obtain, receive, earn, attain; become

give → contribute, donate, provide, supply, offer
take (a bath, a shower, a break, a bus, *exercise) → bathe, shower, relax, ride, exercise

say →state, express, mention, declare

do → exercise, conduct research, study/investigate/research, complete an assignment, commit a crime

make (a thing)→ create, generate, construct, fabricate (false information), manufacture, establish;

make (a promise/vow/commitment) → promise/vow/commit

be (different, bigger, more than, excellent) → differ, exceed, surpass, excel

come out → emerge

meet a problem → encounter, face, deal with, address [an issue, obstacle, difficulty]

have → own, possess something

keep → maintain, sustain; continue

use → employ, utilize; exercise a right

try → attempt, endeavor

show → display, exhibit, reveal

want → desire, pursue, seek

Nouns:

The problem with *people* or any of its alternatives is that they are often used as subjects that are not very meaningful and that shift the focus away from the concepts that really should be the focus. Often, the preferred option when dealing with *people* is not to choose a synonym, but rather to reconstruct the sentence so that a concept is the subject, and *people* can be omitted completely. However, if *people* really ought to be the focus, more specific or more academic words often exist.

people → individuals, residents, citizens, scientists, users, customers, students, educators, leaders.

thing → factor, aspect, category; object, possession; point, aim, goal.

Exercise 1

Improve the following sentences.

a. Most students want to get a good job with a good salary after college.
b. Coming to the US has been a big experience for me.
c. The hardest part of this course was doing the presentations.
d. Many people want to get many things like expensive cars or technological things.
e. I want to take this course to make my grammar better.
f. This lecture will talk about three things: making a program, trying it, and getting rid of bad output.
g. I made a promise to my best friend that I would try to do a good job on my application essay.
h. The big thing that he said was that we need to work hard if we want to do well.

Glossary

abstained: refused

adhere: stick to, follow

adolescent: teen-age

aggravating: annoying

amendment: a change to a law that occurs after it was passed

amplified: make stronger and louder

antibiotic: a drug that kills bacteria

apprehended: arrested

assailant: an attacker

assassinated: killed (a political figure)

atherosclerosis: narrowed arteries

auditory: related to hearing

aviation: flying

awkward: poorly balanced, strange

bankrupt: not having enough funds to pay bills

be analogous: be similar to something

censorship: strict government regulation of speech

collocation: words that usually occur together

colony: a small group trying to settle a new place

commemorate: show respect to a historical figure or event

conceive: imagine

constituents: parts

contemplated: thought about

cumulative: adding up gradually

dangling: hanging loosely

deficiency: lack

delinquent: irresponsible

discerning: figuring out

eliminate: get rid of

eloquent: having lovely speech

emphysema: a lung disease

enzymes: special proteins that speed up reactions

eradicated: completely removed

erroneously: mistakenly

ethical: related to right and wrong

exaggerated: over-emphasized

executed: killed by government for a crime

exuberance: enthusiasm

facilitate: make easier

fertilizer: a substance that makes soil richer

forego: skip

freedom of assembly: freedom to gather

hazardous: dangerous/risky

hesitate: pause not wanting to do something

hilarious: extremely funny

hypertension: high blood pressure

hypothetical: imaginary

ideological: related to political/religious ideas

incalculable: impossible to know the value of

insulated: designed to trap heat

invariably: always

lags: differences in time

lunar: related to the moon

mascot: animal or symbol that represents a group

mature: grow up, become like an adult

melodies: musical tunes

meteor: a large space rock that falls from the sky

notorious: famous in a negative way

nuances: subtle meanings

obscurity: the state of being unknown

overhaul: a change that affects every aspect

patriotic: loving one's country

perpetrator: a person who commits a crime

perpetuates: continues

perplex: confuse

pioneer: a person who does something before others do it

reconciliation: restoring relationships

redundant: repetitive

reservoir: something that stores another thing

rugged: strong, tough

salinity: saltiness

secede: pull away from, separate from

simultaneous: at the same time

stumbled: tripped

subtle: hard to notice

syntax: word order

tempestuous: rough, stormy

tides: the rise and fall of oceans on the shore

transcends: crosses, exceeds

warranted: called for, necessary

Answers Key

Unit 1 Focus

Exercise 1

    a. Immigrants came to the U.S. seeking employment.
    b. American westward expansion was also spurred by immigration.
    c. Industrialization would have been impossible without immigrants to work the factories.
    d. The rugged individualism that marks American culture is also attributable to immigrants.
    e. The patriotism of immigrants also strengthened the U.S.
    f. These days education is a primary goal of those coming to the U.S.

Exercise 2

Sample paragraph:

    Immigration has been essential to the expansion, productivity, and patriotism of the U.S. The large influx of immigrants into the U.S. in the 1800s enabled the U.S. to spread from the Atlantic to the Pacific. Immigrants also worked the factories that were vital to American industrialization. Finally, newcomers to America fueled patriotism because they were thankful for the opportunity to freely pursue their dreams in the U.S.

Unit 2 Triads

Exercise 1

Triads are highlighted in gray.

Dear ELI Friend,

    It is my distinct pleasure both [1]to greet our students when they arrive and [2]to congratulate them at graduation, [3]with, of course, many encounters in between. Almost invariably, I find that the fluent student confidently shaking my hand on graduation day bears little resemblance to the [1]shy, [2]monolingual [3]new arrival I welcomed months earlier during orientation. In the course of time, a radical transformation has taken place, one that transcends the simple acquisition of second language skills. You see, assuming the role of international student is not simply about learning; it's also about becoming. The sojourn from [1]China, [2]Oman, or [3]Colombia does not end with the unpacking of bags in Newark; rather, ELI becomes the point of departure on a deeper journey to the center of the soul. To study in a foreign land is to embark on a quest for identity.
    Consider the case of Shingo, an ELI student from Japan. Speaking Japanese while still in Tokyo, Shingo knew himself and was at ease within the protocols and nuances of his culture. But here in Newark, English opens a door, not simply to new words, but to an uncharted world of uncertainty. [1]Should he bow or shake hands? [2]Should he look down or make eye contact? [3]Does he preserve his silence and humility or

embrace the loud, self-promoting exuberance of his American peers? Finding himself in this new world is like learning to dance to a strange new rhythm. At times, Shingo feels ¹lost and ²anonymous, ³no longer certain of his Japanese identity, while simultaneously sensing he is an imposter among Americans. As the months pass, however, Shingo begins to find his footing—coming to treasure more deeply the ¹beauty, ²order, and ³elegance of Japanese traditions and also finding himself more at ease within the ¹looser, ²freer, ³more fluid dimensions of American culture. He has learned to love and live in two worlds.

This year's edition of our annual newsletter captures how ELI helps students like Shingo evolve into global citizens. The first mark of becoming a global citizen is acquiring the English proficiency to bridge the linguistic divide among classmates from 35 different countries, including, the U.S. The second set of competencies is the ability and willingness to ¹traverse cultural barriers, ²searching for commonalities and ³celebrating differences. Navigating the sometimes tempestuous waters of cultural conflicts requires ¹patience, ²empathy, and the ³courage to set aside time-worn narratives long enough to listen and, perhaps, together write a new story. As Marcel Proust observed, "The real voyage of discovery consists not in finding new landscapes, but in having new eyes."

In the end, however, global citizenship is more than language and cultural understanding; rather it is casting the net of concern and compassion beyond one's borders. ¹It's Saudi scholars going to Puerto Rico to repair homes for the poor; ²it's a Rwandan professional raising awareness among UD undergraduates of human rights abuses and the subsequent healing power of forgiveness and reconciliation; ³it's a Syrian artist collaborating with UD dancers to tell the tragic story of Aleppo, infusing pain with hope. Inside these covers, you will discover remarkable students whose search for identity through their ELI experience proved to be transformative, not only for themselves, but for others as well. Enjoy.

Sincerely,

Exercise 2

a. The weather: Summer weather here is typically hazy, hot, and humid.
b. Your computer: My computer is old, slow, and unreliable.
c. How you feel today: I feel cheerful, enthusiastic, and energetic.
d. Your favorite course: AP Biology is interesting, challenging, and rigorous.
e. Why English is difficult: English is difficult because the grammar is elaborate, the vocabulary is multilingual, and the spelling is often non-phonetic. The grammar includes complicated features such as articles, infinitives, and gerunds. The vocabulary includes words of Germanic, Greek, and Latin origins. Also, the spelling is challenging because there are many ways to spell sounds such as schwa, long vowels, and even f.
f. Favorite foods: The favorite foods of Americans seem to be pizza, hamburgers, and anything with bacon.
g. Common excuses for being late: Students are often late for a wide range of reasons, but the most common seems to be that they overslept, they missed the bus, or that they had to print out an assignment.

Unit 3 Verb Tenses

A. SIMPLE PRESENT

Exercise 1

a. DNA determines which proteins a cell makes. C
b. The market share of Brand ABC expands. I (is expanding)
c. Computers simplify creating documents. C
d. Global temperatures rise since 2000. I (have risen; have been rising)
e. Tulips lose popularity in Georgia. I (have lost; are losing)
f. The topic I choose for my research paper is internet censorship. I (have chosen)

Exercise 2

Chen is a student from China preparing for college in the Unites States. He <u>face</u> many difficulties. He <u>report</u> that simply getting out of bed is difficult because of jet lag. His body clock does not seem to work properly. As a result, he often <u>miss</u> his first class, so he is on academic probation. Another problem he <u>have</u> is that he struggles with daily responsibilities such as fixing meals and cleaning his room. Not eating well <u>make</u> him tired so he cannot pay attention in class, and living in a dirty room <u>cause</u> him to be unproductive, which <u>lead</u> to lower grades. He <u>does</u> not pass his classes this session.

Exercise 3

American college students tend to display speaking habits that often perplex international students. They speak quickly, use slang or vulgar language, and fail to use intonation patterns similar to those of English teachers. Even when internationals excel in their college prep English classes, they still struggle when interacting with American students for the above reasons. English teachers cannot be faulted for speaking more slowly, in standard language, or with proper intonation to communicate meaning. Their job is to teach. The difficulty is mostly attributable to the unique adolescent culture on college campuses. Most college graduates tend to speak in a manner more similar to that of English teachers once they are employed and are compelled to communicate with colleagues older than themselves.

My father lives in an assisted living center, but that does not mean that he is not active or cannot care for himself. In fact, he is very active, as he enjoys golfing and attending a variety of church activities. He loves to sing. He does not tend to talk long on the phone, though.

In the United States, most commuters drive to work unless they live in a metropolis such as New York. There most workers probably take the subway. They may also walk if they live close enough to their place of employment to do so.

Breakfast in the U.S. and breakfast in Japan are quite different. In the U.S., breakfast is often rushed, so cereal, toast, or bagels are common. All of these take almost no time to prepare. In Japan, on the other hand, breakfast resembles other meals in that it often includes fish, rice, and a salad.

B. PRESENT CONTINUOUS

Exercise 1

Sample answers:

a. The clock is ticking, the sun is shining on my feet, and the computer automatic formatting is driving me crazy.
b. Businesses are rapidly globalizing; they are offshoring labor, internationalizing communication, and exported products.
c. My brain is churning through ideas, my stomach is rumbling with hunger, and my fingers are fumbling at the keyboard.

C. PRESENT PERFECT

Exercise 1

This course has already been offered for more than five years. Most students have found it to be quite helpful. Many have even come back to thank me for teaching them. I certainly have enjoyed teaching it and creating a textbook based on the lessons from this course, although a publisher for the book has not been found yet.

1. The present perfect uses are highlighted above.
2. The present perfect was chosen because the course has been going on for several years and still is. She is talking about a time range from the past into the present.

D. MIXED PRESENT TENSES

Professional football **has been** (present perfect) a major sport in the American sports scene for nearly a century, but many international students in the United States **do not understand** (simple present) the game despite the attention that **is being paid** (present continuous) to it by Americans around them. Perhaps the international students do not want (simple present) to learn about football because **the game does not exis**t (simple present) in their home countries. However, the National Football League (NFL) **is considering** (present continuous) expanding to include venues in Europe and perhaps even in Asia. This desire by the NFL to expand overseas may result from the fact that viewership in the U.S. **has decreased** (present perfect) for the past two years.

1. What tense is each verb?
2. Why was each tense chosen? Present is always, continuous is now, present perfect is from past to now.

Sample paragraph:

Volleyball is a sport that was invented in the U.S., but it gained great popularity internationally before it started to expand in the U.S. Right now, volleyball is considered secondary to basketball among indoor sports for men, and few high schools even offer it for boys, but is has become the number one indoor sport for women. Recently, the Olympics has added beach doubles volleyball as a sport, and the NCAA has even more recently added sand volleyball. There is still room for its expansion as a sport, as four-player volleyball on grass is becoming increasing popular. Volleyball teaches interdependence, teamwork that optimizes the unique skills of each player, and communication.

E. SIMPLE PAST

The verbs with an asterisk (*) also require doubling of the final consonant.

Exercise 1

Sample paragraphs:

a. How has the use of technology developed over the past ten years?
It seems like in the past ten years, technology has moved away from the computer toward the cell phone. In short, cell phones have become mini-computers that may even replace desktop and laptop computers. This change strongly favors those with nimble fingers who have grown up with phones.

b. How has your lifestyle changed in the last decade?
In the last decade, my lifestyle has shifted somewhat from participating to serving and teaching others who participate. Ten years ago, I played volleyball in several leagues and even won several local championships, but since that time, I have become a coach and a referee, so I play less. Instead, I serve the families of players I coach, I teach the players, and I serve the volleyball community by officiating matches.

c. How has music changed in the past decade? (See model answer in the Unit.)

d. How have your techniques of studying English developed over the past decade?
Ten years ago, I was interested primarily in teaching English, and that is still my top priority, but my interest in research involving the usage of English words, word frequencies, and research-based teaching techniques is growing. It is that very interest that has led to the writing of this book.

Unit 4. Passive Voice

A. USING THE PASSIVE VOICE

Exercise 1

    a. Vast amounts of research are being conducted worldwide.
    b. The personal information of thousands of government employees was hacked.
    c. Billions of web pages are produced each year.
    d. Cannot be made passive.
    e. More crime is committed by adolescents today than 50 years ago.

Exercise 2

    The process of hearing is somewhat complicated. Sound waves are gathered by the outer ear so they strike the eardrum, which is caused to vibrate. These vibrations are amplified by three bones in the middle ear. The amplified waves are then transmitted to the fluid-filled cochlea, where fluid waves are established. These waves ultimately cause hair cells in certain locations to be bent, leading to the firing of sensory neurons, sending auditory information to the brain, where that information is interpreted.

    a. Passive verbs are highlighted in the paragraph above.
    b. When the author wants to point out what structures perform the functions; When the agents are either obvious or too complicated to describe.
    c. To explain the process of hearing.
    d. To focus on the process more than the structures that play roles in the process.

Exercise 3

Sample paragraphs:

    a. First, rice should be rinsed. Then, the rice is measured into a rice cooker. After that, water is added in a 1.25 to 1 ratio to the rice. Once the lid is placed on the rice cooker, the cooker can be plugged in and turned on. Perfect rice can be served after approximately 30 minutes.
    b. Once food is taken into the mouth, it is chewed and swallowed. The food passes through the esophagus into the stomach, where it is churned physically and digested chemically with acid. Subsequently, it passes into the small intestine, where it is broken down enzymatically into nutrients that are small enough to be absorbed through the intestinal walls.
    c. This one is difficult, as recent experience is lacking. Twenty years ago, HTML code was used for every type of font and format, and it was an extremely tedious process. Surely the process has been simplified since then, but the current process must be explained elsewhere.

B. TRANSITIVITY

Exercise 1

    a. Prices of vegetables were declined in May. <u>I; declined (only)</u>
    b. The number of international students in the U.S. has increased each year since 2007. <u>C</u>
    c. The policy on immigration was changed last month. <u>I; changed (only) would be better</u>
    d. The students discussed about how to divide labor for their group project. <u>I; about</u>
    e. When the plug contacts with the outlet, electricity flows. <u>I; with</u>
    f. The new policy will influence on everything from tuition to curriculum. <u>I; on</u>
    g. It is considered important to reduce all types of waste. <u>C</u>
    h. The book was criticized because it lacked realism. <u>C</u>
    i. Automobiles have been improved considerably in the past century. <u>I; been</u>
    j. Each organism impacts many others, so the value of each one is incalculable. <u>C</u>

Unit 5 Modals

A. GENERAL USE

Exercise 1

Sample paragraphs:

    a. Much can be done to make cars safer, and much actually is being done. Cars can be equipped with sensors that alert drivers to excessive speeds, to other vehicles in blind spots, and to vehicles or other objects in front of them. Drivers can also be educated or tested more regularly. Enforcement of driving laws can also be intensified, especially with respect to driving while intoxicated and texting while driving.

    b. If there were no budgetary limits to the manufacturing of automobiles, they could be programmed to be truly automatic. Cars, like drones, could be programmed to drive themselves with their passengers inside. Driving, would cease to exist. However, such artificial intelligence would be expensive, and it could make the traveling less interesting, especially for those who enjoy driving.

Exercise 2

Sample paragraph:

    To prepare for a trip to Newark, Delaware, not much preparation is required. Of course, the traveler should have all documents such as passports or driver's licenses with them. The weather in Newark is seasonal, but it tends to be mild, so short sleeve shirts for summer should be packed, and coats for winter should also be brought. During spring and fall, sweatshirts should be accessible, but they can be easily purchased. An umbrella should also be brought, as heavy rainstorms are not unusual.

B. HEDGING

Exercise 3

Sample answers:

- a. Trump may be the most controversial American president in the last century.
- b. Boxing might be considered the most hazardous sport.
- c. Education should probably be the top priority for governments.
- d. It might snow tomorrow.
- e. The extinction of the dinosaurs may have been caused by a meteor.
- f. The printing press could be the most significant invention in history.
- g. Cats might be superior pets to dogs because they require less attention and because they do not need to be walked.

Unit 6. Nouns

B. COUNTABILITY

Exercise 1

Non-count nouns are highlighted in gray; count nouns are underlined.

Countability is not necessarily intuitive. Money is not countable even though people count it regularly, while stars are countable even though no one can count them. Some words are even countable sometimes and not countable at other times. Thus, reading and listening are important, and attention must be paid to the countability of nouns.

- a. Yes.
- b. Yes.
- c. No. If you don't have time to do something, it is not countable.
- d. They are counting dollars or pounds, or whatever the currency may be.

Exercise 2
Sample answers

- a. nc: At the grocery store; c: at a restaurant
- b. c: at a restaurant; nc: from the city or out of a faucet
- c. nc: The wide range of general engineering development;
     c: They teach different types of technologies such as information technology, medical technology, and architectural technology.

Exercise 3

a. ~~Many researches have~~ Much research has shown that Vitamin A deficiency causes blindness.
b. The police could not find any evidence that suggested that the victim knew his assailant.
c. The course was beneficial because students gained ~~many knowledges~~ much knowledge.
d. A large-scale investigation was conducted to discover the psychological factors associated with longevity.
e. That course is difficult because of all the ~~homeworks~~ homework.
f. The counselor offered the students many ~~advices~~ suggestions.
g. ~~Informations are~~ Information is easy to access on the Internet.

C. QUANTIFIERS

Exercise 1

a. research <u>a large volume of</u>
b. oxygen <u>a considerable amount of</u>
c. information <u>vast amounts of</u>
d. furniture <u>an abundance of</u>
e. money <u>a large sum of</u>
f. studies <u>countless</u>
g. evidence <u>minute amounts of</u>
h. gasoline <u>large quantity of</u>
i. concepts <u>a wide array of</u>
j. complexity <u>considerable</u>

D. ARTICLES

Exercise 1

[1]<u>A</u> 14-year-old fatherless Japanese boy born in [2] <u>the</u> early 1800s went on to influence [3] <u>ø</u> history significantly. One day, [4] <u>the</u> boy and several of his friends went fishing. They were blown by [5] <u>a</u> storm to [6] <u>an</u> island far from Japan. [7] <u>The</u> storm wrecked their boat, so they stayed on [8] <u>the</u> island several months eating[9] <u>ø</u> crabs, [10] <u>ø</u> fish, and [11] <u>an</u> occasional albatross (a large bird). One day [12] <u>a</u> whaling ship from [13] <u>the</u> United States discovered [14] <u>the</u> boys on [15] <u>the</u> island because [16] <u>the</u> cook on [17] <u>the</u> ship wanted to find [18] <u>ø</u> turtles for [19] <u>ø</u> turtle soup. [20] <u>The</u> boys were taken to [21] <u>the</u> ship, and [22] <u>the</u> 14-year-old eventually reached [23] <u>ø</u> Massachusetts, where he was adopted and educated. Eventually, he returned to [24] <u>the</u> Japanese Islands and influenced [25] <u>(the or ø)</u> political leaders there to sign [26] <u>a</u> treaty of [27] <u>ø</u> peace and [28] <u>ø</u> trade with [29] <u>the</u> U. S. This treaty began [30] <u>the</u> industrialization of [31] <u>ø</u> Japan, which began [32] <u>the</u> modernization of [33] <u>ø</u> Asia. [34] <u>The</u> boy became one of [35] <u>the</u> most influential Japanese men in [36] <u>the</u> history of Japan.

Exercise 2

a. England
b. China
c. Saudi Arabia
d. the United States

e. Walmart
f. the People's Republic of China
g. the Commonwealth of Virginia
h. the City of Philadelphia
i. Maine
j. the Kingdom of Saudi Arabia

k. the Delaware River
l. the Rockies
m. France
n. the Aleutian Islands
o. the Aleutians

Exercise 3

a. He crossed the river, not the state.
b. People and land animals; river animals such as fish.

E. ADJECTIVAL NOUNS

Exercise 1

a. The car stereo is in the repair shop
b. There is a two-week long holiday break.
c. There will be 30-minute student presentations with 15-minute question and answer periods.
d. State driving laws differ.

Exercise 2

Choose the correct word for each case.

a. educational
b. education
c. economics
d. relaxation
e. Geography; geographical

f. reflective
g. safe
h. safety
i. Scientific
j. Science

Exercise 3
Sample paragraphs:

a. Universities contribute greatly to society. They impart knowledge to young adults who will become the leaders of business, government, and science. Perhaps even more importantly, they provide a relatively safe environment for young adults to find themselves and mature intellectually, socially, and psychologically. Moreover, universities conduct basic and applied research that brings about technological development.

b. Technology has affected food considerably. Genetic engineering, for example, has enabled highly nutritious and disease-resistant varieties of crops to be developed. Not only that, but technological processing and packaging enhances the shelf-life of food and enables it to be transported safely. Furthermore, chemical technology provides fertilizers, pesticides, and herbicides which increase agricultural productivity.

Exercise 4

1. ~~The~~ society needs laborers with a high level of education.
2. The police ~~is~~ <u>are</u> coming to gather information about the crime.
3. If lessons can be learned from ~~the~~ history, civilization can advance.
4. The history of the U.S. is not nearly as long as that of China. <u>C</u>
5. 5. ~~The~~ nature is the greatest inspiration for engineers.
6. ~~The~~ life is full of irony.
7. The life of O. Henry was difficult and tragic.
8. Government is a necessary evil: without it, there is chaos; but with it, there are restrictions on freedom. <u>C</u>
9. <u>The </u>American government consists of three branches.
10. An economy based on consumption can be dangerous to<u> the </u>environment.

F. NOMINALIZATION

Verb	Noun	Verb	Noun
accept	acceptance	cover	coverage
accuse	accusation	criticize	criticism
acknowledge	acknowledgment	debate	debate
affirm	affirmation	decide	decision
aggregate	aggregate	declare	declaration
amend	amendment	defame	defamation
analyze	analysis	defend	defense
annoy	annoyance	define	definition
appeal	appeal	demonstrate	demonstration
apply	application	denature	denaturation
approach	approach	depress	depression
approve	approval	derive	derivation
argue	argument	describe	description
assemble	assembly	deter	determination
associate	association	determine	deterrent
attempt	attempt	develop	development
behave	behavior	disagree	disagreement
benefit	benefit	discriminate	discrimination
bond	bond	discuss	discussion
bribe	bribe, bribery	disenfranchise	disenfranchisement
cite	citation	dissent	dissent
claim	claim	distract	distraction
coincide	coincidence	embezzle	embezzlement
commit	commitment	emerge	emergence
communicate	communication	emphasize	emphasis
compare	comparison	equivocate	equivocation

compensate	compensation	establish	establishment
compete	competition	execute	execution
compose	composition	exhibit	exhibition
conceive	concentration	explain	explanation
concentrate	concept	expose	exposure
condense	condensation	express	expression
conduct	conduct	extend	extension
conflict	conflict	flatter	flattery
confuse	confusion	frustrate	frustration
constitute	constitution	generalize	generalization
control	control	generate	generation
convict	convict	grow	growth
cooperate	cooperation	hinder	hindrance
court	courtship	hydrolyze	hydrolysis
implement	implementation	provoke	provocation
impress	impression	publish	publication
imprison	imprisonment	punish	punishment
incite	incitement	react	reaction
inform	information	recommend	recommendation
injure	injury	recruit	recruitment
institutionalize	institutionalization	rehabilitate	rehabilitation
insulate	insulation	reinforce	reinforcement
interfere	interference	release	release
internalize	internalization	represent	representation
invest	investment	reproduce	reproduction
justify	justification	reserve	reservation
label	label	resist	resistance
legislate	legislation	restrain	restraint
manipulate	manipulation	restrict	restriction
metabolize	metabolism	revolve	revolution
modify	modification	rob	robbery
notify	notify	sanction	sanction
observe	observation	saturate	saturation
offend	offense	seduce	seduction
oppose	opposition	socialize	socialization
oppose	opposition	state	statement
organize	organization	stigmatize	stigmatization
participate	participation	store	storage
perceive	perception	substitute	substitution
persevere	perseverance	suggest	suggestion
persist	persistence	support	support
persuade	persuasion	suppress	suppression

pity	pity	tend	tendency
plagiarize	plagiarism	transcend	transcendence
possess	possession	transport	transportation
present	presentation	treat	treatment
preside	president	utter	utterance
promote	promotion	value	value
protect	protection	vary	variation
protest	protest		
provide	provision		

Adjective	Noun	Adjective	Noun
abundant	abundance	homosexual	homosexuality
acceptable	acceptability	hyperactive	hyperactivity
accessible	accessibility	ideal	ideal
acidic	acidity	important	importance
active	activity	inconvenient	inconvenience
addictive	addict	independent	independence
adolescent	adolescence	inevitable	inevitability
alcoholic	alcohol	interior	interior
analogous	analogy	intimate	intimacy
bureaucratic	bureaucracy	just	justice
causal	causality	lazy	laziness
cognitive	cognition	major	majority
complex	complexity	malicious	malice
confident	confidence	moral	morality
consistent	consistency	necessary	necessity
controversial	controversy	normless	normlessness
corrupt	corruption	nutritious	nutrition
credible	credibility	obscene	obscenity
criminal	criminal	polar	polarity
delinquent	delinquency	poor	poverty
democratic	democracy	probable	probability
depraved	depravity	prominent	prominence
deviant	deviance	rational	rationality
difficult	difficulty	residential	residence
diverse	diversity	responsible	responsibility
easy	ease	safe	safety
effective	effectiveness	scholarly	scholarliness
eloquent	eloquence	strong	strength

emotional	emotionality	sympathetic	sympathy
equal	equality	true	truth
evil	evil	violent	violence
false	falsehood	vulgar	vulgarity
free	freedom	wicked	wickedness
frequent	frequency		

Exercise 1

    a. execution
    b. legislation
    c. equality; access; access
    d. abundance; (*vegetation* and *populations* are nominalizations)
    e. eloquence
    f. compensation (*Employers, workers, paying, hospitalization,* and *rehabilitation* are nominalizations)
    g. (noted in d and f)

Exercise 2

    a. Global warming could cause expansion of deserts (desertification), leading to the extinction of many species of animals and plants.
    b. Globalization leads to the shifting of manufacturing operations to locations with cheaper labor.

Exercise 3

Sample paragraph:

In early American society, churches were community centers and the primary agents of social control in small agricultural villages. However, urbanization and industrialization increased social complexity, with public education, courts, and prisons becoming predominant regulators of behavior (Kornblum, 2008). (37 words)

A. VERB + PREPOSITION COLLOCATIONS

I. 1 – 10 are all *to*.

II. 1-10 are all *with*.

    a. of
    b. of
    c. to
    d. to
    e. to
    f. to

III. 1-13 are all *from*.

    a. to
    b. from; to
    c. to

IV. Miscellaneous

    a. Being a woman did not prevent Curie <u>from</u> becoming a great scientist.
    b. The new rule prohibits students <u>from</u> parking in that area.
    c. The speaker challenged his listeners <u>to</u> change the world by voting for his brother, and although he persuaded most <u>to</u> vote the following day, he was unable to convince many <u>to</u> back his brother.
    d. She insists <u>on</u> coming to class late even though her grades are dropping.
    e. He developed his vocabulary by persisting <u>in</u> reading extensively.
    f. The lawyer objected <u>to</u> her client's being questioned in that particular manner.
    g. The swelling resulted <u>from</u> an infection. If untreated, the infection could result <u>in</u> death.

Test yourself

1. to
2. with
3. on
4. from
5. from
6, 7. from; to
8, 9. from; from

10, 11. to; in
12, 13. from; with
14, 15. to; to
16. of
17, 18. to do; from
19, 20. to; to

1. X
2. X
3. X
4. X

5. with
6. on
7. on
8. of

Unit 8. Gerunds and Infinitives

In Sentence 4, *to become* is a <u>noun</u> and it is the <u>subject</u> of the sentence.
In Sentence 5, *to improve* is a <u>noun</u> and it is the <u>object</u> of seeking.
In Sentence 6, *to improve* is an <u>adverb</u>.
In sentence 7, *to welcome* functions as an <u>adjective</u>.

B. PURPOSE PHRASES

Exercise 1

Complete the following sentences with causative or purpose expressions.

 a. The new policy will force <u>automobile owners to pay a special tax</u>.
 b. The instructor permitted <u>students to use their cell phones in class</u>.
 c. The surgery will enable <u>the patient to walk again</u>.
 d. The captain led <u>his troops to attack the fortress</u>.
 e. Her parents inspired <u>her to become a teacher</u>.
 f. The purpose of this exercise is <u>to practice infinitival expressions</u>.
 g. The goal of this course is <u>to enhance writing proficiency in a short period of time</u>.
 h. The aim of the coach was <u>to encourage</u> his team <u>to play tenacious defense</u>.
 i. Global warming may cause the ice caps <u>to melt</u>, which could lead to higher sea levels, which could compel coastal dwellers <u>to move further inland</u>.

C. GERUND OR INFINITIVE?

 11. The doctor could not remember locking the door. That particular day
 12. The doctor could not remember to lock the door. every day
 13. The student stopped to buy coffee. He drinks coffee.
 14. The student stopped buying coffee. He gave up coffee.

Exercise 2

 a. Students should avoid <u>using cell phones in class</u>.
 b. It is important not to hesitate <u>to ask if you have a question</u>.
 c. The law will prohibit <u>allowing engines to idle more than two minutes</u>.
 d. Teachers must not excuse <u>arriving late to class</u>.
 e. A child should not be permitted <u>to be outside alone after dark</u>.
 f. It is difficult to imagine <u>passing this course without a miracle</u>.
 g. International students often complain <u>about having to pay so much for textbooks</u>.
 h. The contract appears <u>to be legitimate, but a lawyer should check it</u>.
 i. The senator did not <u>recall voting for the new tax bill</u>.
 j. The astronauts are preparing <u>to land their craft on the moon</u>.

Exercise 3

 a. By <u>studying hard,</u> I will be able <u>to pass the course</u> without <u>having to find a tutor.</u>
 b. Instead of <u>using a dictionary</u>, students should <u>ask a teacher if one is available</u>.
 c. In order <u>to drive a car,</u> it is necessary <u>to obtain a driver's license</u>.
 d. <u>Receiving a flu shot</u> will prevent <u>contracting the flu most of the time</u>.

D. PARALLEL STRUCTURE WITH GERUNDS AND INFINITIVES

Exercise 4

Sample answers:

    a. I remember <u>skating, losing my balance, and falling</u>.
    b. The school does not allow students <u>to wear jewelry, get tattoos, or wear shorts</u>.
    c. Doctors do not advise <u>smoking, drinking excessively, or being sedentary</u>.

Exercise 5

Sample paragraph

    My mother passed away nearly twenty years ago, but I remember her enjoying reading the Bible and talking with church friends. She avoiding driving anywhere because she never obtained a driver's license, so entertaining friends at home was perfect for her. My mother encouraged me to work diligently and to pray, and to see God working in the simple activities of life. I remember her teaching me to be polite, use the proper tone of voice, and to never talk back to her. I also remember with great distaste her washing my mouth out with soap when I uttered a rude and impertinent obscenity.

Unit 9 Subjunctives

Exercise 1

Sample paragraph:

    The Main Street shopping area requires renovation in a variety of ways. It is first recommended that the street itself be re-paved, as it has numerous potholes that endanger cars and pedestrians. Furthermore, it is suggested that the sidewalks either be rubberized or be heated to prevent Icing over in the winter. It is also recommended that a community center with a gym and free parking be built to bring new vitality to Main Street.

Exercise 2

Sample paragraph:

    In this day of environmental pollution and global warming, it is vital that consumerism be seen as risky, and that a new attitude of minimizing waste be adopted. It is essential that unnecessary products simply not be produced or purchased. Furthermore, it is crucial that products be re-used, if at all possible, before being disposed of. It is also critical that recycling of paper, metal, and plastic become mandatory, and that technology to recycle textiles (clothing) be developed. There is only one earth, and the importance of preserving it cannot be overstated.

Unit 10 Adjectives and Adjective Clauses

A. ADJECTIVES

Exercise 1

a. I; stressful
b. I; dangerous
c. I; were aware of

d. I; relaxing
e. C
f. I; annoying

    5. X
    6. X

Exercise 2

a. It is easy for students to commute by Uber.
b. It is difficult for parents to raise their children when they both work.

D. THAT VS. WHY, WHERE, AND IN WHICH

Exercise 3

a. that
b. that
c. Both are possible, but they have different meanings. "that" means she was the pilot; "in which" means she was a passenger.
d. where
e. that
f. that
g. in which

E. REDUCING ADJECTIVE CLAUSES

Exercise 4

a. (e). The restaurant she enjoys most is The Blue Heron.
b. (f). The assignment due yesterday was easy.

Exercise 5

a. The boy who was running to catch the train passed many office workers.
b. The boy passed many office workers who were running to catch the train.

F. SUCH AS

Exercise 6

   a. Chronic illnesses such as atherosclerosis, hypertension, and diabetes are all related to obesity.
   b. Most student dorm rooms contain snack foods such as tortilla chips, crackers, or cookies.
   c. Families tend to gather on holidays such as Christmas, Thanksgiving, and Memorial Day.
   d. Sports such as sumo, volleyball, and soft tennis are popular in Japan but not in the U.S.

G. DEFINITIONS

     A pickle is a cucumber or other vegetable [1]that has been soaked in a solution[2] that is so high in salinity, acidity, or both that bacteria cannot grow. Pickles have shelf-lives [3]that far exceed those of fresh vegetables, so pickling is a practical way to provide food in the winter. Pickles also pack flavor [4]that far exceeds their volume because of the salt or acid [5]in which they have been soaked. Therefore, they are often used on sandwiches or in salads [6]sold in delis.

Exercise 7

   a. 6
   b. One was reduced; the last one
   c. 1 and 2

Exercise 8

Sample paragraphs:

   a. A supervisor is a person who oversees other workers. The supervisor is often the person who has the most experience at the job or who has had special managerial training. Effective supervisors can help identify workers who are ready for promotion and those who may need to be fired. They can also ensure the productivity that the company needs to be competitive.
   b. A hamburger is a sandwich that usually consists of a ground beef patty with some toppings on a bun. It is an item that is often sold at fast food restaurants. Perhaps the restaurant that is the most famous for hamburgers is MacDonald's, but its popularity seems to be waning with the recent push for healthier food.
   c. A vacation is a period of time during which workers vacate the office. Is it a time that is looked forward to, and many workers engage in vacation activities that are fun but stressful. A common complaint heard after vacations is that the workers are happy to be back to work, as it is a vacation from their vacation.
   d. An emergency room is a place in a hospital that is reserved for patients who need immediate care. They are usually equipped to treat life-threating events such as heart attacks, poisoning, or car accidents. It is a place that is commonly seen in TV dramas because of the intensity involved in its activities.
   e. A passport is a document that must be obtained to travel abroad. To acquire one, documents such as official identification, proof of address, and special passport application forms must be submitted to the government office that is in charge of issuing passports. The process

may take months, so it is essential to plan ahead and begin the process early.

    f. The greenhouse effect is the name given to the process by which CO_2 accumulates in the atmosphere, acting like a blanket, and causing atmospheric temperatures to rise. Another term that is associated with the greenhouse effect is global warming.

Exercise 9

Sample paragraphs:

    a. I will never forget the day when I first saw the Japanese women's volleyball team playing in the Olympics on TV. The team ran a fast, powerful offense with quick middle hits and was characterized by a tenacious defense that dove for every ball and did not let the ball hit the ground. During a break, a special look into the practices of the team was provided, and the intensity of the practices impressed me incredibly. From that day on, I took an avid interest in volleyball.

    b. I once met an inspiring person who encouraged me to become an English teacher. He was an English teacher in China, and he stayed with me for a few days when he returned from China for a brief vacation. My encounter with him helped me realize that I enjoyed work that involved internationals, and that I could probably teach English in China or some other nation that needed me.

H. MODIFYING CLAUSAL MEANING RATHER THAN A WORD

Exercise 10

    a. Sentence 30 is clearer.
    b. Sentence 29 is more efficient.
    c. Clarity is generally more important.
    d. Generally 30 is better, but if words are limited or if a paraphrase is needed, 29 is useful.

Exercise 11

Sample sentences:

    a. Trump won the presidential election of 2016, <u>which surprised almost everyone.</u>
    b. Global temperatures continue to rise, <u>which calls for more action to limit CO_2 emissions</u>.
    c. Stock market prices have risen consistently since 2016, <u>which means it is advantageous to invest now.</u>
    d. A new antibiotic-resistant bacteria has been discovered, <u>which means that new antibiotics must be developed, and that until such antibiotics are available, deaths from infection are likely</u>.

Unit 11 Coordinating Conjunctions and Transitions

B. COMMA SPLICE RUN-ON SENTENCES

3. Ducks swim, they also fly. X

B. USING SIMPLISTIC TRANSITIONS

Exercise 1

Sample paragraphs:

a. Living in a dormitory brings a number of clear advantages to students. These advantages include proximity to classrooms, easy access to dining halls, and convenient opportunities to make friends. However, these advantages are often offset by disadvantages, the first of which is cost. Generally speaking, a student can live less expensively off campus. Also, while access to dining halls is convenient, it also seems to be correlated with weight gain, so many students choose to move off campus for health reasons. In addition, while dorms offer opportunities for friendships, they are also noisy and may interfere with study.

b. Given a choice whether to drive or walk somewhere, most Americans would choose to drive without a second thought. Driving is quick and easy, and it enables transportation of objects as well as passengers. Nevertheless, driving has important disadvantages. It is expensive, with payments for insurance, gasoline, parking, and the car itself. It is also environmentally unfriendly. Car exhaust ruins the air, as citizens of Beijing, Mexico City, and Los Angeles can testify. Walking, on the other hand is healthy, thought-stimulating, and clean. It takes time to walk, but the benefits of walking relative to driving are undeniably worth the time.

c. These days fast food is often in the news for its relationship to obesity and other health issues. However, when fast food originated, it brought several advantages. It was delicious, filling, and convenient, especially for travelers. In the early days of fast food restaurants, they played an important role for those who were on the road. No one went to fast food restaurants on a daily basis. However, with economic prosperity, consumers could afford to go out to eat more frequently, and the desire for delicious food with no preparation time or dishes to clean led the public to overuse fast food. At that point, the disadvantages appeared: hypertension, obesity, and heart disease.

Unit 12. Comparisons

Year	Korean	Chinese	Saudi	Colombian
2000	50/50, T = 100	2/0, T = 2	1/0, T = 1	15/20, T = 35
2008	30/30, T = 60	40/10, T = 50	20/5, T = 25	10/15, T = 25
2016	5/5, T = 10	150/100, T = 250	80/40, T = 120	5/5, T = 10

Exercise 1

    a. In 2008, there were four times as many Chinese men as Chinese women at IU.

    b. There were five times as many Chinese students at IU in 2016 as in 2008.

    c. The total number of Colombians at IU in 2016 was less than one-third that of 2000.

    d. In 2008, there were 50 times as many Korean students as Chinese students at IU.

    e. In 2016 there were equal numbers of Columbian men and women.

    f. The number of Saudi women increased eight-fold from 2008 to 2016.

    g. There were only one-sixth as many Korean men at IU in 2016 as in 2008.

Exercise 2

One major trend was that there [1] were [2] fewer Korean students in [3] 2016 than in [4] 2016 at IU. The trend was [5] similar for Colombians. The Korean population decreased by 90 [6] percent, while the Colombian population decreased by [7] more than 60 percent.

Exercise 3

Sample paragraph:

On the other hand, Chinese and Saudi populations at IU showed the opposite trend. The Chinese population showed a 125-fold increase, while the Saudi population displayed a similar 120-fold rise.

B. COMPARISONS WITH OUT- VERBS

Table 7: Useful academic out- verbs

outnumber	outclass	outrun	outrank	outproduce
outweigh	outlive	outplay	outlast	outsmart*
outperform	outsell	outscore	outvote	outwit*

* *smart* is an adjective, but outsmart is a verb, so it is included in this table.

* wit is a noun, but *outwit* is a verb

Exercise 4

    a. Performed better than; earned higher grades than

    b. Cast more votes than; won the election

    c. Be smarter than; trick

Exercise 5

    a. The goal of any manufacturing company is to outproduce and outsell its competitors.

    b. Surprisingly, the BMW did not outperform the Honda in road tests.

    c. Battery A outlasted Battery B by 25% in the experiment.

    d. Longevity data reveals that in general, women outlive men by 5 years.

    e. The advantages outweigh the disadvantages.

f. Usain Bolt easily <u>outran</u> the competition in the 100-meter dash.
g. That luxury hotel simply <u>outclasses</u> this roadside motel in every way.
h. The champions <u>outplayed</u> their opponent convincingly and <u>outscored</u> them 6 to 1.

Exercise 6

Sample answers:

a. In 2000, Korean students outnumbered Chinese students by a ratio of 50:1.
b. However, by 2016, the situation was reversed, with Chinese outnumbering Koreans 25:1.
c. Nevertheless, with respect to GPA, in each case, the smaller group outperformed the larger.

Unit 13 Adverbs and Adverbial Clauses

A. INCREASING EFFICIENCY WITH ADVERBS

Exercise 1

a. In the stomach, food is digested physically and chemically.
b. Politicians should utter statements that are politically and factually correct.
c. Children of illegal refugees tend to struggle educationally, economically, and socially.

B. HEDGING WITH ADVERBS

Exercise 2

Sample answers:

a. Sugar is arguably a dangerous food ingredient.
b. Virtually all medicines can produce unhealthy side-effects.
c. Practically every lawyer faces ethical dilemmas.
d. Jimmy Carter was perhaps the most misunderstood president of the twentieth century.

C. BOOSTING WITH ADVERBS

Exercise 3

Sample answers:

a. Obviously, water is essential for life on earth.
b. Education definitely deserves a greater portion of the budget.
c. Being absent assuredly leads to failure.
d. Dogs are certainly smarter than cats because they can be taught obedience.
e. Greater English skill clearly leads to higher salaries, whether the English is a native or a second language.

D. FRONTING NEGATIVE ADVERBS

Exercise 4
Sample answers:

    a. Not only can animals communicate, but some can also use tools.
    b. Rarely does it snow in Florida, but when it does, orange juice prices skyrocket.
    c. Only once has her husband apologized for forgetting her birthday.
    d. Seldom does this class have assign homework that cannot be finished in fifteen minutes.
    e. Not until the 1990s did personal computers become popular, but once they did, the growth of the computer industry sparked an economic boom.

E. ADVERBIAL CLAUSES

Exercise 1

    a. I; Due to the snow that
    b. C
    c. C
    d. I; a fragment. …to remove the snow, they didn't finish by morning.
    e. I; eliminate *but*
    f. I; change *during* to *while*
    g. C
    h. C
    i. C
    j. I; dangling participle. While watching the falling snow, residents heard sirens throughout the city.

Exercise 2
Sample answers:

    a. Everywhere the president visited <u>well-wishers turned out to greet him</u>.
    b. The bridge was built so (that<u>) commuters could save time traveling between two major cities</u>.
    c. Although writing assignments are difficult, <u>they are essential to developing writing skill</u>.
    d. Because the president had promised to reduce taxes, <u>she was popular</u>.
    e. When <u>the student fell asleep in class</u>, the instructor <u>simply ignored him</u>.
    f. Although many enjoyed the new movie, few <u>provided compelling reasons why they liked it</u>.
    g. Despite the fact <u>that ice exists on Mars, no life forms have yet been identified</u>.
    h. Up until now, <u>students have been allowed to park in the B lot</u>, but from now on <u>they will be ticketed for doing so</u>.

Unit 14 Conditionals

C. PAST CONDITIONALS

Exercise 1
Sample answers:

a. If humans did not have to eat, <u>they could accomplish more</u>.
b. If cell phones are found to cause cancer, <u>lawsuits will surely result</u>.
c. If fossil fuels run out, <u>renewable forms of energy can be used</u>.
d. Unless children are educated, <u>they will not become effective employees</u>.
e. If cancer research receives greater funding, <u>a cure for the disease might be found quickly</u>.
f. If Yao Ming had not played in the NBA, <u>the basketball boom in China might not have occurred</u>.
g. If bacteria did not exist, <u>decomposition would not occur, and soil would be less fertile</u>.

Exercise 2
Sample paragraphs:

Choice 1:

    If fossil fuels run out, renewable forms of energy can be used. The technology for harvesting the energy of the wind and sun exists. Solar and wind energy can play a major role in replacing fossil fuels. Cars can run on solar energy; some models exist already. Wind energy can be used to supplement nuclear energy to power cities.

Choice 2:

    If bacteria did not exist, decomposition would not occur, and soil would be less fertile. Infertile soil would lead to crop and vegetation failure, which would lead to starvation and reduction of all animal populations. In short, without bacteria, life itself would probably not exist.

A. EVEN IF AND EVEN THOUGH

Exercise 3
Sample answers:

a. Even if the course is difficult, <u>I will enjoy it because the topic and instructor are fascinating</u>.
b. Even though the doctor wrote a prescription, <u>the patient failed to obtain the medicine from the pharmacy</u>.
c. Even though the plane took off on time, <u>it arrived two hours late, to the dismay of its passengers</u>.
d. Even if simultaneous language translating devices are invented, <u>there will be a need for language experts</u>.
e. Even if the Apollo spacecraft had not landed on the moon, <u>some other spacecraft would have eventually done so</u>.

Unit 15. Noun Clauses

Paragraph 1

It is well known [1]that the longest days of the summer occur around June 22 in the Northern Hemisphere, and [2]that the shortest days of winter occur around December 21. It is also commonly recognized [3]that the hottest days of summer north of the equator typically do not occur until late July or even August. Similarly, it is often observed [4]that the coldest days of winter do not usually occur until February. However, [5]why the lags between extremes of day length and extremes of temperature exist is seldom contemplated. When asked about this phenomenon, most college students reply [6]that they do not know. The principle that explains the day length/temperature phenomenon is [7]that the earth acts as a heat reservoir. When the days are the longest, the earth absorbs heat, removing it from the atmosphere. The result is [8]that in June, the air temperature is relatively cool. Then in late July or August, as the days shorten, the earth releases its heat, causing the atmosphere to be warmed by both the sun and the earth, resulting in higher temperatures. In winter, when the days are the shortest, the earth continues releasing its heat until February, which is [9]when the coldest temperatures occur.

What roles in the sentences do they play?

1. Complement	2. Complement	3. Complement	4. Complement
5. Subject	6. Object of verb	7. Complement	8. Complement
9. Complement			

Exercise 1
Sample answers:
    a. It is difficult to understand <u>why peace seems so elusive</u>.
    b. Few would have predicted <u>that Trump would be elected president</u>.
    c. Few parents realize <u>how sensitive yet adaptable children are</u>.
    d. I often wonder <u>whether life exists on other planets</u>.
    e. It is clear that <u>popular tastes in music have changed dramatically since 1950</u>.
    f. It is unclear <u>whether or not the course will run next semester</u>.
    g. <u>What causes cells to become cancerous</u> is what researchers need to find out.

Exercise 2
Sample paragraphs
    a. Many opponents of fast food believe that it should be banned. They claim that it is a public health hazard and that as long as they exist, the public will need to spend untold billions on health care. However, those opinions seem to be extreme. Most studies have shown that fast food on an occasional basis poses no clear risk to health. The key to fast food, as with anything else, is moderation. If the public is sensible, there is no compelling reason to ban fast foods.
    a. Some believe that space exploration should be a high priority, stating that the earth is overpopulated and that global warming or nuclear holocaust might cause the earth to become uninhabitable in the future. This pessimistic opinion, though extreme, seems to

understand that human nature seems to cause this race to destroy itself. If such is the case, space exploration would only be a postponement of the inevitable. Humans would destroy any other planet as well. Funds and attention would be spent more effectively seeking solutions that enable humans to be less destructive.

Unit 16. Reported Speech

B. DIRECT QUOTES

Exercise 1

  a. I; no citation
  b. I; *presents* cannot take *that-noun clause; his idea that*
  c. C
  d. I; misplaced period; it goes after the citation.
  e. C
  f. f. C
  g. I; *wrote*
  h. I; *criticizes* cannot take a that-noun clause; delete *that*.

Exercise 2

Sample paragraph:

  Dungy seems to be a broad-minded coach who espouses a perspective on coaching that sees sports as what they are – games. He does understand that the job of the coach is to enable the team to win, as he uses techniques such as the "look squad" (p. 2) to allow his team to visualize opponents and how his team's strategies might work against them (Dungy & Whitaker, 2011). Nevertheless, he claims that player development, character, and integrity are more important than winning, and he seems to criticize players and media that value perception rather than reality. He boldly asserts, "Perceptions don't win ball games" (p. 12).

Dungy, T., & Whitaker, N. (2011). *The one-year uncommon life daily challenge*. Carol Stream, IL: Tyndale Momentum.

Unit 17. Approaching an Academic Voice

Exercise 1

Sample answers

   a. Most students seek fulfilling, high paying jobs after college.

   b. Experiencing life in the U.S. has transformed me.

   c. Presentations were the most difficult part of the course.

   d. Expensive cars and technological gadgets are sought by many.

   e. This course develops grammar.

   f. This lecture discusses three primary concepts: creating a program, running it, and debugging it.

   g. I promised my closest friend to endeavor to write an excellent application essay.

   h. His main point was that diligence leads to success.

About the Author

Kenneth (Ken) Cranker studied biology, concentrating in human nutrition, at Cornell University. It was while working in a biochemical laboratory there that Ken came into contact with international post-docs conducting top-notch research in English, a non-native language, and he was inspired to become an ESL teacher. After obtaining an M.S. in TESOL at SUNY Albany, he taught in Japan for twelve years, nearly half of which were at the university level. After returning to the U.S., he has been teaching primarily English for academic purposes at the University of Delaware English Language Institute, preparing conditionally admitted students for university studies.

Wayzgoose Press publishes a popular line of self-study ebooks for students of English as a second language. Find the full range of current titles, including guides for practicing reading, writing, grammar, speaking, listening, grammar, and vocabulary, here on our website.

To be notified about new titles and special contests, events, and sales from Wayzgoose Press, please visit our website at http://wayzgoosepress.com and sign up for our mailing list. (We send email infrequently, and you can unsubscribe at any time.)

88385961R00066

Made in the USA
Lexington, KY
11 May 2018